I0083215

Wholeness of Being

You are Source—infinite consciousness.
Everything else is your story.

Written by

Floris V. J. de Clercq

ALL RIGHTS RESERVED

No part of this book may be reproduced or transmitted in any form whatsoever, electronic, or mechanical, including photo-copying, recording, or by any informational storage or retrieval system without express written and dated permission from the author.

Wholeness of Being

© 2014 *by Floris V. J. de Clercq*

Editing & Layout, Cover Design by Sebastian Märker

ISBN: 978-3-00-044596-5

For more of Floris V. J. de Clercq's teachings, videos, podcasts, CDs, workshops, and retreats, please visit:

www.wholenessofbeing.com
or
www.inspiration4awakening.com

Acknowledgments

In my early twenties, I was introduced to the Tao Te Ching, Buddhism, metaphysics, and the Infinite Way teachings of Joel Goldsmith. All of these teachings had tremendous influence in my everyday life and my personal awakening.

To Sebastian Märker, thank you for editing this book and for all your love and support.

Floris V. J. de Clercq

Contents

Wholeness of Being

Preface

The wholeness of being is the awareness that everything is Source, appearing as the completeness of itself. It is reality experienced without the conditioned filters of the mind. Learning to anchor our reference point of awareness in Source allows us to see and experience an unfiltered reality. Thinking and doing from the reference point of the ego's fragmented mind leaves us in an unfulfilled cycle of survival and suffering. However, thinking and doing from the reference point of Source awareness is experiencing completion and fulfillment.

Floris reminds us that we are here to experience this life as a glorious adventure. He makes it clear that all the power in the universe exists within us as our very own life force.

The infinite Source that we are is the very same Source that is present and expresses as everything within our awareness. While we are plugged into the collective mind and focused on the human experience, we can only be consciously aware in one life at a time. If we are awake within the dream called physical reality, we are fully aware of the interconnectedness of all life. With this knowledge comes the understanding and responsibility that we do everything to ourselves.

There is only Source expressing as everything within the dream. Everything else is our personal interpretation of the story called life.

PART I

Awakening from the Dream

The Violent Awakening

It was the year 1988; I was living in Johannesburg, South Africa. During this time, I was working for a theater company located a couple of blocks away from where I lived. One late afternoon while I was walking to work, a gang of thugs attacked me. Like a pack of wolves, these men appeared out of nowhere. They leaped onto my body, beating and kicking me until I collapsed. It was like a feeding frenzy with me as the bait. I was overpowered and helpless.

Eventually I could not feel the pain of the punching, the kicking, and the angry, hateful words projected at me. In a state of helplessness, I surrendered to the moment. My fear disappeared, and nothing mattered anymore. Through the chaos of punching fists and kicking feet, I caught a glimpse of the man whom I presumed was their leader. In the moment our eyes met, he leaned over toward me and grabbed my chin to pull my head back. From this angle, I saw a long knife in his hand. He shouted, "We are going to kill you!" The rest of what he said was not clear as darkness enveloped me.

Suddenly, I was awake and fully aware of what was happening, but I was not in my physical body. I was expanded awareness. It was like everyone and everything, including the whole commotion, was happening within my consciousness. Then the noise and shouting faded into an incredible silence. There was no "me" or "them," no details, just the light of images and forms. Everything was interconnected. I was the awareness of this silence, this infinite stillness, and the light appearing as everything.

It seemed like a very long time passed; then through the stillness came a clear whisper: "You do everything to yourself." Suddenly there was a bright flash, the light faded into darkness, and shouting voices in the background interrupted the stillness. I felt a cold heaviness and realized that I was back in my body. The moment I opened my eyes, the attackers stopped shouting and jumped away from me. They appeared shocked or surprised. I was not going to wait around to find out what their story was. Covered in blood, I scrambled to my feet, pushed past them, and ran to the theater, where I found help.

That evening, as I was lying in bed aching from head to toe, I realized something extraordinary had happened that I could not explain. I had experienced that part of me that is timeless and omnipresent, without form or dimension. Instead of feeling traumatized by the event, I felt a sense of peace and fulfillment.

The clarity of this experience revealed that consciousness is not a product of the body, but that the body exists within consciousness. It confirmed that the physical world is a dream: a mind-made reality created of light and experienced through the body-mind as the images and forms of physical reality. The revelations that unfolded from this experience awakened a tidal wave of questions for which I could not find adequate answers. My search activated an inner drive to explore and discover who we really are and what our story is.

Focused, Present Stillness

In my quest for answers, I opened myself up to learn about the various opinions, ideas, and beliefs that were available outside the boundaries of conventional thinking. Along the way, I studied Western and Eastern philosophies, archetypal thought systems, and a variety of various ideas with different spiritual teachers.

As we all eventually learn, knowing and saying we understand something is very different from applying and practicing it. It is impossible to adopt a new way of living if we are still stuck in old habits and rigid belief systems. Most of us only add more information to old conditionings and wonder why nothing seems to work or get better.

To wake up is to realize that we live our lives through the filters of our conditioned minds. Everything we think we know or believe is experienced through filters created by our programming and conditioned beliefs. They influence our perceptions of reality and everything we do; how we react or respond to people, places, and events; and why we resist change. Teachers and philosophers can only give us an intellectual outline of how to see past our filters or how to realize them, but they cannot make anything happen for us. We have to discipline ourselves and do the work if we want to see or experience results.

Just as we don't become doctors or engineers overnight, we also don't awaken or become consciously aware, whole, fulfilled, or enlightened after attending a couple of self-development courses, awakening experiences, or reading books related to these subjects. Being aware and awake within the dream called life takes a lot of undoing and letting go of old paradigms and beliefs that trap us in a fragmented consciousness.

An essential key to awakening is focused, present stillness. Until we have mastered this level of awareness, the best way to learn, practice, and maintain it is through regular stillness meditation. My violent awakening had shifted my perspective of reality to another level of awareness. I yearned to recapture the experience of the infinite stillness and the interconnectedness of everything. For many years prior to the violent awakening, I had practiced various methods of meditation. However, my focus shifted to stillness meditation, and it became an important discipline within my daily routine.

Being present and aware in stillness allows us to transcend the filters of the corporeal mind. Through this practice, we naturally become more aware of the ego's attachments to the stories and illusions within the game of life. Through stillness meditation, we eventually realize that suffering, lack, limitations, problems, and our perceived enemies are all filters. In other words, these perceived experiences are conditioned beliefs and ideas that blur the real picture of wholeness. Our consciousness will never evolve to higher levels of awareness until we realize that our perceptions and perspectives are filters. We will never be free of suffering, lack, limitations, or problems until we reach the level of awareness where we are able to look beyond the filters through which we see and experience our world.

Discovering the ego's "me"

Realizing we have filters is the first step toward conscious living. The next step is to be aware of the ego's identification with and attachment to the material "me." The conditioning we receive within the environment where we evolve programs us to believe that we are separate from everything else within our perceptual awareness. The material "me" is the ego's attachment to separation, division, and the struggle to survive.

From the reference point of the ego, the physical world revolves around the needs, desires, and the incomplete perspectives of the material "me." The feeling of separation and incompleteness always leaves the ego's "me" feeling unfulfilled and the victim of its own story. It cannot live without love, attention, approval, recognition, and validation from others. Without having these needs constantly fulfilled, the ego's material "me" feels rejected, cast out, betrayed, and let down. It feels incomplete.

The side effects of the self-pity of the "me" can result in addictions, anger, resentment, hate, jealousy, and various other self-destructive behaviors. Taking the "me" out of the story is probably one of the most difficult accomplishments for the fragile, self-serving ego to attain.

The ego's material "me" loves living in its conditioned comfort zone. Change or letting go of attachments feels like death. The ego reacts and responds with resistance and becomes defensive against any situation that might shift or challenge its perspectives.

Despite this, the ego is an essential part of our existence within the collective physical reality. However, its purpose is to be an instrument through which we can experience the fulfillment of wholeness and use it to create a harmonious individual reality. If the ego remains anchored in the material "me," then an unfulfilled emptiness results in suffering and the ongoing need for external validation and approval. Surrendering the ego's "me" identification is a slow process that takes time, commitment, and discipline, but most of all, it requires a greater level of awareness.

During the process of recognizing, questioning, and undoing the conditioning of the ego's self-sabotaging "me," I discovered the true art of forgiveness and gratitude. This introduced me to self-healing and redirected my life onto a new path.

Forgiveness and gratitude returns us to wholeness. Practicing it shows and teaches us that our world is a projection and reflection of ourselves. What we see, believe, love, hate, and judge in others is merely a reflection and projection of our own fear, lack of understanding, prejudice, ideas of love, desires, and needs. Forgiveness and gratitude make up the first stage of taking the "me" out of our stories and recognizing that we are all interconnected. This is the first stage of realizing that we are the stillness and the awareness behind our beliefs and thoughts. Life within the collective mind reality is a game where we play (or are played). However, if we are consciously aware of the game, life becomes an adventure of our own choosing, and the game loses its power over us.

I had not yet transcended the game. As much as I thought I had, I was still fighting for survival. To make things worse, I had reached a point where I hit rock bottom—on not only a business or financial level, but also personally. In my struggle, the ego's "me" would occasionally rise to the surface and crack under the perpetual challenges and pressure of my personal needs and the fight for acceptance and recognition. I realized how easy it was to fall back into old, fearful habits and patterns.

To my advantage, I was aware of my conditioning, so I could recognize negativity and the game that my ego's "me" was playing. However, my life was about to change as everything collapsed around me, opening a door to a completely new world.

The Paradigm Shift

For twenty-five years, I had dedicated much of my time seeking greater levels of awareness, training my mind and body to accomplish anything I set out to do. Despite having achieved all my desires, I still felt this unfulfilled emptiness within me. I tried to fill it by increasing my workload and becoming more successful in business. Before I knew it, I was consumed by the hungry systems of materialism and achievements to the extent that I lost touch with my inner stillness. My need for "more" backfired.

I worried continuously about reaching my goals or making enough money to cover my living costs. At the same time, I was heading for burnout, and despite all my enthusiasm and effort, the levels of my business and finances had reached all-time lows. In frustration and not knowing what to do, I made an important decision. Instead of allowing depression and anxiety to control me, I turned to silent meditation. I gave up seeking answers with my intellect and surrendered to the stillness within.

I began dropping my resistance to the changes that were happening and started to allow inner stillness to guide me. Within a year, many changes and synchronistic events unfolded—one of which was my relocation to Europe. Even in my wildest dreams, I had never thought I would end up in Germany. After all, I did not speak or understand the language. However, the whole process unfolded effortlessly. Before I knew it, we were apartment hunting in my partner's hometown: Erfurt, central Germany.

During this time, we were staying with my mother-in-law, who also lived in Erfurt. It was a busy week consisting of getting our immigration papers in order and looking for a suitable apartment. On the specific day when the paradigm shift happened, we had been taking it easy. While the rest of the family was preparing lunch, I used the time to meditate.

I was relaxing on the living room couch, staring up at a mobile of butterflies. My mind was clear and present, my body relaxed. In an empty moment, everything in the room, including my body, disappeared. There was no sense of a physical reality anymore, yet I was fully conscious and awake. It was as if my consciousness had flipped to another level of awareness. There was nothing, just present stillness. I was the awareness of everything and nothing at the same time.

It is difficult to describe this experience, because it is beyond words and language, but I will attempt to give an idea of what happened. Within this blank state of timeless awareness, a faint sound appeared that began to move. This vibration formed light; the light moved. And as it moved, it began creating images and forms that expanded into endless fields of light. I was the nothingness at the center of everything. Then everything contracted into a single point of awareness. From this reference point, I became aware of a faint outline of a room and a body lying on a surface. As I focused in on the body, I saw that it was mine. Suddenly there was a bright flash of light and then darkness followed by a feeling of heaviness.

I slowly became aware that I was in my body. At this stage, I buzzed with an intense vibration. My hands and feet felt cold, and my senses were intensified. I opened my eyes and saw the butterfly mobile hanging above me. What had appeared as a timeless experience, I later realized, had happened within a couple of seconds. My first thoughts were, *Wow! There has either been a glitch in the matrix, or I have briefly experienced being unplugged from the collective mind universe.* It was not a dream, but more like an awakening from a dream. The experience was euphoric. It left me with a heightened sense of awareness and a feeling of fulfillment, joy, and wholeness.

As I sat up on the couch, I experienced an incredible sense of love and gratitude pouring out from the center of my being. It felt as if my heart was exploding with love. Everything in the room appeared as if it was part of me. I had just experienced a shift from body-mind to Source awareness. Before the paradigm shift, I was just an individual person, aware of being in a room with furniture. Now I was the awareness in which the room, furniture, and individual person were present.

Within the next couple of weeks, it felt as if a light had switched on in my head. All the years of reading and studying spiritual teachings and philosophies, from the *Bible* to the *Tao Te Ching*[1], Buddhism, and the Infinite Way[2] teachings of Joel Goldsmith, began to make sense. A new perspective and awareness emerged. I realized I had been spending way too much time trying to intellectualize and analyze all these teachings.

I was active with a lot of "doing" and "thinking," but the one thing I had left out all along was "being"—being present as the Source, which expresses as the doer and the thinker. I realized that as thinkers and doers we become so focused and entrapped in the *doing* and *thinking* of physical reality that we disconnect from *being* who we really are.

With experience, we awaken to the awareness that all knowledge and harmonious ideas flow from inner stillness. If we anchor ourselves in this inner stillness, we can experience and tap into knowledge, ideas, and great discoveries. Source awareness is present inner stillness. This is the zero point of all that is, the nothingness expressing as everything. Source is the true nature of our being. In this state of expanded awareness, we are unplugged from the filters of the collective mind and the

---

[1] *Tao Te Ching*. This is an ancient Chinese text apparently written or recorded by Lao Tzu (Lao-zi).

[2] Joel Goldsmith (1892–1964), an American spiritual teacher, healer, author, and mystic, was the founder of the Infinite Way movement.

images and forms that appear as our physical universe.

My violent awakening had revealed to me that consciousness is not a product of the body, but that the body exists within consciousness. However, my paradigm shift experience revealed that although we are this infinite consciousness expressing as every life perceivable, we are only consciously aware in one life at a time.

The paradigm shift awakening was a major turning point in my life. It opened a door to another level of awareness. Before this experience, I had had it all backward. My misunderstanding was that I was trying to be one *with* Source, trying to connect *with* it. After the experience, I realized we *are* Source—infinite consciousness. We are not separate or apart from it. There is nothing to look for or to find. The moment we try to align *with* or pray *to* a perceived higher intelligence, power, or authority, we separate ourselves from it.

This separation has caused confusion and suffering for thousands of years and has kept us distracted and focused on the external, material reality. I realized that if we anchor our awareness in the present stillness of Source, we allow our body-mind to be a transparency, an instrument through which Source radiates and expresses as the wholeness of being.

The paradigm shift awakened me to a completely new perspective on the world, and within the next couple of months, I felt like a new reality was unfolding. I began to see the wholeness of being in everything around me.

We Are the Central Suns of Our Own Universes

Moving to Germany was a culture shock at first. It took practice, patience, and commitment to learn a foreign language and integrate into a new culture. Whenever I felt my ego rising up and pushing with resistance, I would always hear this inner voice whisper: "You have to take the 'me' out of the story." I was learning to see and experience my world from the reference point of Source awareness.

I realized that maintaining this level of awareness is almost impossible if we have not understood that the body-mind (ego) is only an instrument, not our Source. The ego thrives on resistance, and it always pushes itself to the front in times of stress or change, but it is our responsibility to be consciously aware of its activities. Learning to define everyone within our awareness as an expression of our infinite self takes a lot of discipline and letting go of conditioned ideas and beliefs. The hardest lesson for the ego to learn is to accept, allow, and love unconditionally those who do not accept, allow, or love us.

The feeling of fulfillment, wonder, and joy returned to my life. Clear insights and thoughts began to pour through my meditations and dreams. I realized that every one of us is the central sun of our own universe. Whatever we shine our light on grows within our awareness. It became very clear to me that how we perceive and interpret reality is how it appears as our world.

If our focus is on wholeness, joy, love, and a commitment to uplift, we find ourselves in a world that matches these opportunities. However, if our focus is on the misery of misery and the suffering of suffering, then our reality will reflect the miseries of a suffering world.

The point is, what we project reflects back in full. We have the choice to change our perspectives: how we see and experience our world. In the collective mind reality, everything is about perspective, interpretation, and association. The illusion is that we experience everything as separate from us. Through physical eyes it appears that way, but in essence, we are all interconnected. Everything and everyone is an expression of one infinite consciousness: Source.

My paradigm shift experience brought clarity and answers to many unanswered questions. It also demonstrated that we are Source beings plugged into the collective mind reality through the body so that we may have individual experiences. Our journey here is not to suffer for some belief that promises immortality after we die. We are in essence immortal, not as individual beings of flesh and blood, but as infinite consciousness—timeless, omnipresent Source.

As individual beings, we are contracted, focused points (souls) of infinite consciousness (Source). To experience the physical realm, we awaken within the collective mind reality wearing physical bodies. Each individual body experiences the collective from a different perspective. As we look through our bodies' eyes, the experience of the collective mind gives us the perception that we are separate from everything else that is within our awareness.

The collective mind turns everything upside down: we interpret a perception of separation as living in the world instead of the world existing within our consciousness. This interpretation that we are separate from everything initiates the need to survive and the desire for purpose and fulfillment.

We are each present in these bodies to experience a unique perspective of the collective mind reality. This life can be an adventure or a burden. Whatever we choose determines how we interpret this experience and the outcome of how it unfolds.

My many years of practicing stillness meditation— contemplating and surfing the highs and lows of the collective mind reality—has made it clear that we are Source expressing as physical bodies. As Source beings, everything we could ever want or need is already present, complete, whole, and available in every time frame of reality we can perceive. However, before we can be conscious of the wholeness of being, we first have to unfold to that level of awareness.

I would like to share my insights and experiences

with those who are seeking clarity and a more in-depth awareness of who we are. The remainder of this book consists of my personal realizations and inspirations and the life lessons I have learned, tried, tested, and experienced over the last thirty years of seeking and teaching. I also include some questions and answers from seminars or workshops. I can only write what is true for me, what feels right, and what I have experienced and practiced in my life.

There is nothing in this book for you to "believe in." All the power in the universe exists within you. Through present stillness, you have access to it. You do not need to be in a sacred place or space. Infinite Source is present as you, wherever you are. No one else can give it to you or take it away. You simply have to transcend your filters and allow it to shine through you.

I do know that if you have the discipline and patience to be present, awake, and aware within your inner stillness, you will eventually discover that you are Source—infinite consciousness. Everything else is just your story, created by your thoughts, ideas, and beliefs.

PART II

Exploring Who and What We Are

Everything Is Source

My various life-changing experiences revealed to me that there is only *Source* and *the story*. Source is infinite consciousness, and the story is the dream we call physical life.

What is Source?

Source is incorporeal intelligence, the nondual singularity present as the substance of all life. Source is nonfocused consciousness: the formless, timeless awareness from which everything appears. It is infinite consciousness expressed as the life and light forming all of creation.

Every unique life experience is Source expressed as an individual, focused point of consciousness (soul). The soul is a powerful individualization of Source, which forms a field of energy, allowing a biological universe of life to evolve, form, and shape the body-mind (corporeal vehicle). The body of every individual is the vehicle through which Source experiences a unique perception and perspective of the collective mind. We are Source—

infinite consciousness simultaneously appearing and expressing as every life perceivable—but, again, we can only be consciously aware in one life at a time. Source is the nothingness that appears as everything perceivable.

Where is Source?

Source is the only presence; it appears as life happening in the present moment of "now." Everything else is the flow of dreams that manifest as thinking and doing within the corporeal mind of every individual. Source is infinite life, present as the awareness of all probabilities and possibilities. It cannot be in one place and not another; it is present in all places at the same time.

There is no separation or division (duality) in Source. We cannot worship or pray to Source, because it is not a concept out there somewhere. Source is not separate from anything that has consciousness, because it is the consciousness of everything. Source is present as every individual living being, dreaming a story within the collective mind reality.

The Infinite *I* and Soul

I compare the relationship of soul and Source to that of the wave and the ocean. I hope that this will help bring clarity to the subject.

When we watch the ocean, it is obvious to us that the wave (soul) is not separate from the ocean (Source). Thinking that we are souls who are separate from Source, or that we need to connect or align with Source to become whole, is like thinking the wave is separate from the ocean. The wave does not have to *do* something to align or connect with the ocean, because it is just an effect of the wind and natural forces acting on the water's surface. Through these forces, the surface of the ocean expresses as a wave in the same way as the natural laws of the collective mind allow an individual expression of Source (soul) to express as a form (body).

The soul is not separate from Source. It is a focused point of Source appearing within the collective mind. Source does not make the body or fix anything; in the same way, the ocean does not make, control, or fix the wave. The ocean is just "being" the ocean in the same way that Source is just "being" Source.

Our identification with and attachments to our individual perspectives on reality result in the sense and belief that we are separate from everything we perceive in our universe. However, we are not separate from anything; our minds just interpret it that way. We are all expressions of Source. This is similar to thinking that each wave in the ocean is separate from another.

When we shift our focus and expand our awareness to the bigger picture, we realize that there is only the ocean and not separate waves. We are under a similar illusion when we have our reference point of awareness focused and anchored in the fragmented perspective of material reality. In the human experience, this happens when we attach to and identify with the images and forms of individuality. This deludes us with the perception that we are separate from everything. We cannot grasp the bigger picture through the filters of our minds, because the filters fragment our perspectives on the world. We have to transcend our filters and anchor our awareness in present stillness before the illusions of separation and division dissipate.

Can I influence Source for my own needs in any way?

No! Any attempt to influence or manipulate Source to fulfill your needs or desires makes it clear that you still believe you are separate from it. Many of us forget this part when we pray to a "higher power" for love, better relationships, money, or health. The higher power is present as *us*. It has never left. We will never find it anywhere else outside of our consciousness.

Source is not separate from us. Our true nature of

being is Source, the nondual substance of all life, expressing as the light that our minds and senses interpret as the world of form. Everything we want or desire is already present, but we first have to match its specific vibration before it unfolds or appears within our physical reality.

For years, I have been praying for help, for better health, and more money, but nothing has happened. What am I doing wrong?

Source is not aware of our individuality, just as the ocean is not aware of the individual wave. Source cannot give us health, wealth, or prosperity. Source expresses through us as our world. Therefore, we have all the power to choose how we perceive, interpret, and associate ourselves with the collective we live in. Our choices determine what we see and experience as our reality.

Source has no awareness of mind-made problems and does not experience lack, disease, fear, or limitations. In the same way, the ocean does not have an awareness of the wave's perspective of crashing on the rocks. For example, if we have no money in our bank accounts, praying to Source is not going to fix the problem. Source is already complete and has no awareness of our problems. Everything that appears incomplete is a product of our fragmented minds and the way each of us interprets the collective. Perceived problems are self-inflicted; they are only perceptions created within our individual stories through our own beliefs and conditionings. To change our personal circumstances, we have to recondition or reprogram our perceptions and perspectives: how we interpret our world and how we associate with it.

Let us go back to the ocean-wave analogy for a moment and imagine that each wave has an individual personality. In other words, the wave has attached to and identified with its superficial form and has forgotten that it is the ocean (Source), expressed as an individual wave (soul). In this example, if the superficial wave awakens to realize it is more than just an empty shape and is a complete wave (soul) that is an expression of the ocean (Source), then it will experience the richness and magnificence that the ocean has to offer. The same happens for us when we become aware that we are Source appearing as all life. From this moment or realization, we get to experience the abundance, prosperity, wealth, and joy of the wholeness of being.

The Purpose of Perception

Source does not have purpose; it just "is." Source is singular, nondual, formless, infinite, and omnipresent.

Therefore, there is nothing to attach to or identify with. Only within the dualistic perceptions of a mind-made reality can we attach to and identify with something. This dual perception is what creates and generates the collective mind program when we awaken within physical bodies.

The goal of perception is to experience the conscious joy of dreaming an adventure within the collective mind. However, when we identify with our perceptions, the dream consumes us and we forget who we are. Through questioning, contemplation, and meditation, we eventually recognize that our perceptions are just filters. As we wake up to this realization, our perceived attachments, all forms of resistances, and the feelings of suffering dissolve. Furthermore, we also realize that we are only dreaming this reality and that everything within it is an outer projection of the inner self reflecting back to us.

Levels of Awareness

What is corporeal mind awareness?

We are born with incorporeal awareness, but as our brains and physical senses develop, our reference point of awareness becomes anchored in the corporeal mind. The separation from incorporeal awareness is a gradual process. It happens as we begin to recognize, attach to, and identify ourselves as bodies. In humans, this shift of awareness happens at about the age of one or two. It is the beginning of the ego's journey as a conscious individual.

The patterns of repetition, conditioning, and programming we receive within the collective we evolve in become the filters through which we experience the collective mind reality. At this stage, we have entered the game of life. The idea of this adventure is to develop awareness within this dense reality until we realize that life is a game. From here, we transcend to playing the game instead of being played. However, just knowing how to play the game does not mean we are awake. Being awake within the game of life is recognizing that we are the awareness that is aware of the player playing the game.

What is incorporeal awareness?

Incorporeal (Source) awareness is the nondual singularity, the infinite timeless awareness, that is present at the center of all the different levels of corporeal awareness. Source is the substance of all life. Therefore, it remains at the center of everything. Incorporeal awareness is the present stillness behind our thoughts. When we unfold to this stillness, we experience the awareness of the infinite self. There is nothing or no one out there except our awareness reflecting or mirroring our perception of reality back to us.

How do we know if we have attained Source awareness?

If we try to *attain* Source awareness, it means that we are still separate from it. In this state of fragmented awareness, Source awareness will never happen. Being present in the stillness of inner being, beyond the activities, filters, images, and forms of mind-made reality, is "being one with" all that is. This is Source awareness. Here we experience the completeness and wholeness of being.

If you have difficulty "being" present in stillness, I recommend that you first start practicing a basic breathing meditation technique. It is as simple as focusing and following your breath. Your state of mind holds the key. *Be* focused on wholeness and completeness; *be* present in attentive awareness, and *be* your breath. This will open the door to inner stillness. You will know when it happens, because stillness is alive. You have to experience it. Trying to intellectualize or fake it is not possible; the proof is always in the experience.

Present stillness is not going to happen in a couple of sittings. It takes time, dedication, and freeing yourself from the mind's conditioned filters that anchor your perception of reality in separation and resistance. Try it. Practice breathing meditation and discover present stillness. Learn to go beyond the conditioned filters of the mind and discover an infinite reality without boundaries and limitations.

The Collective Mind

You are always referring to the collective mind. What is it?

Through practicing present stillness, I became aware that the collective mind is a dream environment, a program in which Source expresses as images and forms through the filters of perception. The collective mind is where our stories happen. It is the realm where awareness is experienced and where demonstration and desire mold the game of life.

The collective mind reality appears through our individual consciousnesses as the material universe. It can also be perceived as a multidimensional hologram or a collection of evolved systems and laws similar to a matrix. Einstein's mathematical formula for mass-energy equivalence ($E = mc^2$) shows that everything in the material universe is made up of energy.[3] All mass is energy, and energy particles vibrate. Every thought, idea, or belief has a vibration and frequency. The collective mind is the vibrational universe, the realm of all

[3] $E = mc^2$: Mathematical formula for mass-energy equivalence by Albert Einstein (1879–1955), first published in 1905 in his *Annus Mirabilis* papers.

probabilities and possibilities. It reacts, responds, reflects, and projects back to us what we feel and how we perceive our world. Our brain converts the vibrational information within the collective into a three-dimensional experience. Therefore, the conditioning and programming we receive within the environment in which we evolve limits our corporeal awareness to the perceptions within that specific part of the collective.

Everything within our corporeal mind reality is relative to the level of awareness within the collective mind we exist in. Through questioning our conditioned ideas and beliefs, we can shift to new or expanded levels. Here we can explore different vibrational dimensions and frequencies that were previously not in our awareness. However, we resist any change, progress, or chance to expand awareness if we remain stuck in an old paradigm with the agenda to defend our rigid, limited perspectives.

Every being is a contracted, focused point (soul) of infinite consciousness (Source), expressing and experiencing through a body-mind (vehicle) a unique perspective of the collective mind. As focused points of Source, we are plugged into the collective through which we experience a unique perception of the same material universe, worlds, landscapes, people, and creatures. The collective mind is like the program within the body-mind consciousness that allows us to experience a physical reality. The only way we can unplug from the collective is through focused, present stillness.

It All Happens in the Mind

The collective mind is alive. It is a vibrational multiverse of mind-made realities consisting of many collectives, programs, and systems. Within each individual collective, there are many different levels and dimensions vibrating at different frequencies. Evolving and intelligent life exists everywhere within the collective multiverse. Every thought, idea, or concept perceivable is possible because it is perception that creates it. Remember, this all happens within our individual consciousnesses. Through our corporeal vehicles (body-minds), we plug into the collective, where we experience the physical universe and play out our stories. If we unplug from the collective, we experience present stillness, the zero point where mind meets Source. From this still point, we have access to our entire universe.

If all of these dimensions and realms exist within our consciousness, how can we access them?

Many teachings refer to these dimensions within the collective mind as "spiritual" realms. They only appear that way to us because we are on a different frequency. We cannot be aware or even conscious of them if our vibrational frequency does not match that specific level of awareness.

A radio is a simple analogy: there are many different frequencies (stations) we can tune into, each one offering a different experience. Once we have tuned into a specific station, we cannot hear the others or even be aware of them. We have to return to the radio tuner (present stillness) if we want to change stations.

The collective mind is like the radio; it has many frequencies that offer countless opportunities to experience different realities. If we are aware of the radio and the tuner, we can tune into whatever adventure we desire. Remember, these are our stories. Our lives as we experience them happen within our consciousness. So we can tune into different vibrations and frequencies with the way we use our minds. What we think, believe, feel, and focus on shifts us to the reality that matches their specific frequencies.

There is a way to relocate our awarenesses to other frequencies if we so desire. Remember, your true nature of being is Source—infinite consciousness, the stillness in which the collective mind game happens. So, if you want to find the ultimate tuner that can take you to any station on the radio (collective mind), be present in the stillness of your inner being. Find your zero point. Source does not have dimensions and realms; only the collective mind does. But do not forget that Source is present at the center of every experience within the collective, regardless of its vibrational frequency.

From the stillness of Source, you can tune into any

story you desire. If you are aware that the game happens within your consciousness, then you are aware enough to choose how you want to play out your adventures. Remember, there is only Source; everything else is your story created by your thoughts, ideas, and beliefs.

What allows me to experience this physical body, and why do certain situations and events happen to me and not to others?

The program that you plug into within the collective mind you evolve in influences everything about you. The collective mind gives you the experience of physicality and the perception of a material universe. The natural laws that have evolved to form the collective govern everything that evolves or appears within it. Everything, from a single cell to a fully developed being, is a product of the collective mind.

From the reference point of your corporeal mind, the reality you experience within the collective is similar to a hologram. It always matches the vibrational frequency you hold as your awareness of reality, reflecting your beliefs through the people, places, and situations around you. In other words, your individual or collective focus allows people, places, and events to manifest into your reality as good, bad, or neutral. If your perception of the world is fragmented and filled with negativity, you resist progress and remain locked in the lower frequencies, resulting in suffering and discordant experiences.

However, everything within the collective mind is based on perception. Therefore, in reality, the qualities of good, bad, or neutral exist within your beliefs and nowhere else. Everything you are aware of happens within your consciousness. It is only your belief that something happens to you and not to someone else.

I have been sitting in silence for years and nothing special has happened. Why not?

In stillness, nothing happens. The whole point is to be present as the nothingness that expresses as everything. The expectation that something might happen when you meditate prevents anything from happening. If there is something that you would like to manifest or experience, focus on it with excitement and an intensified feeling of achievement *before* you do your stillness meditation.

Present stillness dissolves your conditioned filters, allowing the mind to be an instrument through which Source expresses as the things, ideas, and dreams you focus on. Never go into your meditation with expectations, because that distracts you with perceptions instead of allowing you to be a transparency for Source. Everything is already complete and present, but you have to unfold to that awareness and then anchor yourself in stillness.

Keep practicing breath and stillness meditation. When you have surrendered to the moment, you will experience the interconnectedness of life on every level of awareness. Then, you will recognize the wholeness of being. All power is already within you. It is your story. Therefore, no one can make it happen for you.

Remember, expanding awareness has two parts to it. The first is developing our ability to focus, which enhances our intelligence and opens us up to a new perspective and perception of the collective mind reality. The second part is to develop our capacity to *be* present in stillness without the interference of a chattering mind. Both are essential disciplines for awakening.

Natural Laws

How do natural laws fit into the wholeness of being?

Everything that appears in nature is a perfect expression of infinite consciousness. All life existing within the collective is formed, interconnected, and governed, by natural laws. Nature in its perfect state is a reflection of unconditional love appearing as the wholeness of being. We see this in mathematics, geometry, music, and biology.

All living creatures, evolved and evolving, are creations resulting from the natural laws that make up the collective mind. Nothing that appears to exist within the collective can function separately or is immune to the changes and effects of the natural laws. The collective mind is the dream, the program, within our consciousness, where all probabilities and possibilities exist.

Wholeness of Being

What is wholeness of being?

From the perspective of our true nature of being, which is infinite Source, we are already whole and complete in every way possible. Wholeness of being is the conscious awareness that everything is Source, appearing as the completeness of itself.

Through the perception of time, experience, the right questioning, and meditation, we awaken to realize that we are infinite consciousness, the timeless awareness behind our thoughts and everything we perceive. As we learn to rest in present stillness, we begin to see through and past the layers of conditioned filters within our minds. When this begins to happen, we awaken to Source awareness. In this state of *being*, we are conscious that what we perceive as the physical reality is a dream experienced within the collective mind. *Being* present in stillness is the experience of completeness and allows the mind to be an instrument through which Source expresses as the wholeness of being.

How does it feel to experience the wholeness of being?

Through present stillness (Source awareness), we transcend the conditioned filters of the mind. In this state of consciousness, we experience the interconnectedness of all life. This is the wholeness of being, where everything is complete and perfect just as it is. Through the perspective of the corporeal vehicle, this experience results in feelings of fulfillment, oneness, completion, and unconditional love.

The Ego

Source is the omnipresent, timeless, formless awareness appearing as the wholeness of being. The mind interprets Source as light. This is the light that appears as all of life, bringing change and new ideas to the dreamer who is plugged into the collective mind that dreams a physical reality.

Darkness can only exist where there is no light. Darkness is the illusion of separation from Source, from the one presence. It is the fragmentation of wholeness. The moment we identify ourselves as separate, individual beings, the conditioning and programming we receive within the collective mind reality becomes a darkening filter through which the world appears fragmented. In this darkness, the corporeal mind's sense of separation gives birth to the ego.

The ego attaches and identifies with the perception that we are our bodies. In this state of awareness, we have no conscious comprehension of Source. However, we do have an innate feeling of emptiness urging us to search for wholeness, fulfillment, and completion. This is the soul communicating with us, letting us know that there is more to life than what we experience through the five senses.

The catch is that most of us are so focused on the ego's fragmented perspective of the world that we interpret these feelings as lack and need. Instead of going within and *being* present in stillness, we seek fulfillment in the superficial world of perceptions. Here we follow belief systems and worship mind-made gods who exist in other realms. Alternatively, some of us glorify the physical images of famous people who we believe have found fulfillment and completion through materialism. While we are stuck in the perception of time, space, and the natural laws of the collective mind, the ongoing search for completion and fulfillment leads us in circles.

We will never be free of the constant search for fulfillment until we realize that we are seeing and experiencing our world through conditioned filters that prevent us from realizing the clear picture of wholeness. From the ego's reference point of awareness, we only ever see our own shadows and reflections in everything we perceive; hence our ongoing battle for survival. As long as we believe that the mind is the creator, healer, and master of the physical world, there will always be suffering, lack, and unfulfilled desire.

Can I get rid of the ego?

No. Why would you want to get rid of the ego? The ego is an essential and necessary instrument that helps you to experience the contrasting realms of the collective. You cannot have this physical life without it.

The important point is to be consciously aware that the ego is not your master or controller, but instead an instrument that is there to serve you. All human beings, regardless of how aware and awake they assume themselves to be, are vulnerable to the ego's fluctuations between positive and negative judgments. The more aware we are of the games it plays, the less power it has over us, but denying the ego's existence is always the biggest downfall for anyone, including those who are teachers of truth. We see this happening with spiritual teachers and leaders who claim to be all pure and free of the ego, but eventually, their shadow sides are exposed and they fall from their pedestals.

No one in a physical body is pure and flawless. This vibrational realm is too heavy for that. There are no superhumans. The idea that there can be is a deceptive trick of the ego. It gives us a false sense of power that we are better, above, or more advanced than other beings. Some beings might appear to be more aware or intelligent than others, but that is due to circumstances that have unfolded for them within the collective story. However, we are all the same Source; we just wear different space suits and have uniquely different experiences from others perspectives of reality.

We all have the same power available to us whether we are aware of it or not. This power is the true nature of our being: Source. Our level of awareness determine how Source unfolds as our reality, giving us the opportunity to learn, grow, and evolve as physical beings.

Why is life so easy for some people and extremely difficult for others?

Ego-life in the collective mind reality is like a surprise package. We do not always know what we are going to get. We have to use every opportunity and make the most of the adventure. The one advantage that we all have, which levels the playing field, is that we are all the same Source, the same infinite consciousness. The sooner we awaken to realize that all the power, creativity, and joy of life exists as us and is present as the true nature of our being, the sooner we can recognize it in the world we perceive around us. This is the experience of heaven on earth. Regardless of the type, color, or shape of our corporeal vehicles, everyone is the one and same Source, experiencing a unique perspective of the collective mind reality.

Recognize that your true power is infinite and know that your interpretation of your world is the reality you create. You hold all the probabilities and possibilities within your own attitude. If you know this, you will never again say that someone else has it easier than you do. It is your story; you decide.

The Ego's Game

I come from a very important and powerful family. Apparently, we are more spiritually advanced than other people are; this is why we incarnate into these important families. How do you see this from your perspective?

The darkest game the negative ego plays is to persuade beings, whether as individuals, groups, or cultures, to believe that they are more spiritual than other people are. No being, human, monarch, ruler, alien, or anything we could believe ourselves to be is spiritually above or below, less or more evolved, than any other being—irrespective of race, culture, bloodline, appearance, or qualifications. The latter are merely ways of identifying our uniqueness, programming, and conditioning within the collective mind reality.

We are not the images and forms we appear as; we only use these bodies as vehicles to play within this game. Our true nature of being is infinite consciousness: Source—no less and no more than any other human being.

Hierarchical divisions are all part of the survival games played within the collective mind. They give the ego a false sense of material power over other beings. Only the ego thinks it is more important than someone else is. The point to remember is that you are here to experience this life as an adventure. Whatever you do to people and how you treat those around you, which includes your thoughts about them, is purely a reflection of your own complete or incomplete self. There is only Source. Everything else is your story.

I have been trying to use mind power to manipulate situations around me, but I am failing miserably. A friend of mine said that mind power is not the real power that makes things happen. She said that the mind is only a tool. What is your opinion?

When we, as individual beings, awaken to the awareness that there is only one presence—one Source appearing as the wholeness of being—then we realize that the corporeal mind itself has no power. The power does not come from the mind. The true power is Source, the life and substance of all that is. The mind, when used as an instrument of focus, allows Source to radiate through its filters, manifesting the intentions and desires of the individual.

Source expresses through us as the completeness and wholeness experienced within the collective. Remember, the collective mind reality happens within our consciousness. Hence, everything we manifest in our world happens through us and not to us from somewhere outside. Our states of mind, beliefs, and feelings have an enormous effect on what manifests in our lives as our reality. In other words, whatever we believe and focus on with intent and feeling unfolds as our reality, regardless of our character.

For example, some of us are kind and generous, but we may have issues, beliefs, and negative programming about wealth and prosperity. Our emotions around these concepts sabotage our attraction of abundance. What we believe about our world and the values we give to the material things within it affect how we attract the things of the world to us.

Here is another example to the other extreme: some of us are very rich and constantly manifest more wealth, prosperity, and everything we desire. The difference here is believing that wealth and abundance are good, essential, and easily accessible. Hence, in this case, manifesting more of whatever we want is effortless. How we use our minds and the way we interpret our world and experiences within the collective influences the way our reality unfolds.

Regardless of our conditioning or beliefs, we are all the central suns of our own universes. What we shine our light on becomes visible within our reality.

I once had an awakening experience. Do I have to continue doing meditation and awareness training?

Some of us believe that once we have experienced an awakening or a so-called alignment with Source, we do not need to continue the discipline of practicing self-reflection and stillness meditation. However, an unfocused and undisciplined mind anchored in the ego's perception of a fragmented world can be very disruptive and can trick us into believing we are awake.

Everything in the corporeal mind-world takes time and practice. No one becomes a master in anything by having one awakening experience. We have to unlearn and reprogram our perspectives of the world because it is very easy to fall back into old, conditioned habits.

Truly awakening is like developing a muscle. It takes many hours of focus and discipline to be present in stillness; just meditating is not enough. The other essential part to awakening includes practicing heartfelt love. This has to do with recognizing and acknowledging that every being is infinite consciousness—Source. Living the wholeness of being is living consciously in Source awareness.

The Soul and Its Purpose

The true nature of our being is incorporeal intelligence. We are infinite, formless, omnipresent consciousness. In other words, we are Source. Every unique life experience is Source expressed as an individual, focused point of consciousness. This powerful individualization of Source is the soul.

The soul is a gathering point for consciousness that allows an entire universe of biological systems to evolve and develop within its field, forming the corporeal vehicle. The aura is the soul's field. It cannot be seen with physical eyes. This is because human sight is restricted to a very limited range of the light spectrum. However, the aura can be felt by those who are sensitive enough.

The aura is an energetic field of vibrational information about each physical being. People with a heightened sense of awareness and ability to feel can read or interpret these fields. This is rare, though, because most people are desensitized and distracted by the ego's conditioned filters.

All the countless incarnated beings appearing within the collective mind are souls (individual expressions of

Source). Every soul is plugged into the collective mind, which allows it to have a corporeal vehicle through which it can experience a unique and separate perspective of the material reality. In other words, we are all of life happening, but we are only consciously aware in one physical life experience at a time.

Why do we need souls?

As infinite consciousness, the soul allows us to experience individuality, which initiates the sense that we are separate and divided from everything else. Without the soul, we would not have the opportunity to plug into a mind-made reality where we can create unique experiences and explore the perceptual realms of density.

Our physical bodies automatically anchor us in a corporeal perspective of the collective mind. However, once we awaken to the awareness that we are incorporeal Source experiencing a corporeal reality through the filters of the mind, the game within the collective begins to change, and we begin to live life consciously. From that moment, we can choose how we would like to play the game instead of the game playing us.

Self-Identification

As individual beings, our self-identification happens in our first and second year of life when we begin to associate and identify ourselves with a physical form and image.

Our transition to self-identification and the attachment to the material "me" happen gradually. As babies, we start shifting from *being* to thinking and doing. Through this process, we become self-identified as individual people, which gives us the perception that we are separate from everyone and everything else within our awareness. Identification and attachment with the material "me" kicks in. Our reference point of awareness shifts from Source awareness (the infinite *I*) to the physical sense awareness of the corporeal vehicle.

Through the conditioning and programming we receive within the collective mind, we become mesmerized by the images and appearances of the world. This anchors us in the corporeal mind reality. Here we lose our inner sense of who we are and remain disconnected from the true nature of our being. However, the process of forgetting is essential to our survival and evolution as humans.

Awakening doesn't happen for everyone. For many of us, the program we plug into within the collective holds us mesmerized with distractions, activities, and challenges to the extent that we remain slaves to the mind's perception of reality. This is just another choice.

No one *needs* to wake up. Doing so does not make anyone less or more spiritual than someone else. However, being consciously aware of who we truly are behind our physical masks unfolds a more harmonious, joyous and prosperous adventure.

Finding Fulfillment

The feeling of incompleteness and the need for fulfillment is the soul's way of informing the ego that there is more to life than just the physical and materialistic perspective. Fulfillment is the experience of wholeness and completeness. It cannot be found in the external realms of perception and materialism. Nothing in the mind-made realms of the collective is complete or whole. Every form and image is a temporary expression within the illusion of time. The only true experience of fulfillment within the collective is the awareness that we are Source—infinite consciousness, being aware of our completeness. We can only be aware of this through present inner stillness.

The ego finds the idea of inner stillness fearful. It cannot relate to it because it occupies itself with survival issues and other distractions. Trying to still the mind feels like a death threat to the ego's obsessive mind activities. If we have never experienced the wholeness or completeness of present stillness, we spend our lives searching for fulfillment through external gratifications, materialism, and all the illusions of the mind-made reality.

No matter how much our ego achieves or accomplishes, we fail to find fulfillment, so the search continues until death or self-realization. Every experience, good or bad, happy or sad, is an essential step toward self-realization and the unfolding process of awakening to our inner stillness. Sometimes it takes disaster, loss, and total surrender before we find our way. The adventure is different for everyone, but one thing remains the same: inner stillness unplugs us from the distractions of the collective mind reality and allows us to be present as Source, the true nature of our being.

Why do we have to suffer and have all these uncomfortable experiences?

Without the contrast of the dualistic, corporeal world, we will never really know the true feelings of joy, happiness, love, and gratitude—or the taste of chocolate. The contrast between the experiences of love, joy, and harmony and the uncomfortable realities of suffering are part of the deal. They are the reason that we began questioning our perceptions of reality. If everything were an experience of constant blissfulness, then we would not need to evolve or question anything that feels uncomfortable.

Once we have questioned our thoughts, ideas, and beliefs thoroughly, we realize that there is nothing left except our stories. The next step is to realize that we are not our stories but the stillness out of which they arise. Through this present stillness, we experience the completeness of everything: the wholeness of being.

As we begin to live in joy, love, and gratitude, the feelings of wholeness dissolve the dark filters of the ego, allowing the light of Source to flow through us as great inspiration. Everything is possible when we live in and have our reference point of awareness in Source. The advantage is that it helps to create a more pleasant life adventure.

The Evolving Collective

How does the collective mind benefit from me living this physical existence?

From the perspective of the collective mind, the purpose of the soul experiencing a physical life is beneficial to the expanding and evolving consciousness. The greater collective mind is the collective consciousness of all thoughts, ideas, and experiences. Every new perspective adds to its expansion and evolution. Each generation benefits from what the previous generation has learned and experienced. The fluctuation of highs and lows brings out the best and worst in humans. This is essential for the process of growing, learning, and evolving.

It is like playing an intricate computer game where every decision and move you make with your assigned character (corporeal vehicle) adds to and expands the data bank of information within the game (collective mind), allowing it to calculate more intricate maneuvers and situations. Within the game are many rules, seen and unseen; therefore, the more focused, centered, and aware a player is, the easier it is to understand and play the game.

Therefore, anyone with a heightened sense of awareness has an advantage over those who are stressed and desensitized. The collective mind benefits from every new and unique perspective and experience. Hence, the concept of evolution becomes an important part of the natural laws, governing the greater collective mind reality. You and every being experiencing life within the collective is an important asset to the evolving multiverse. How you choose to play out your adventure is your choice.

Oneness

After the paradigm shift, I realized that we cannot grasp oneness with the mind. It is not an idea or a belief. Oneness is *being*. We can create a language around it or try to teach or explain it, but that would only give us an intellectual idea. Experiencing oneness for ourselves is essential. This is only possible through the expanded awareness of present stillness, because in stillness, we unplug from the perceptual activities of the collective mind reality—allowing us to be present as Source awareness.

The problem arises when we have an idea or image of what we think oneness should be like, because in that moment, it becomes an intellectual concept instead of a heartfelt experience. The true experience of oneness is felt through the heart's center. It is through this center that we are connected to everything within the collective.

As a young man, I had many glimpses of oneness, but in my ego's defensiveness and fear of the unknown, I built a wall of resistance to anything that was not logical to the physical senses. I could not integrate the vastness of oneness as my true nature of being. It took many years of questioning and seeking, including two very contrasting experiences, to shift my perspective of reality, revealing that the infinite "I" was and is always present as everything I was looking for.

This realization enabled me to anchor my reference point of awareness in Source, allowing me to experience the perspective of the dreamer consciously. When I realized that the physical body is just a vehicle with no real power of its own, I began to experience strong resistance from my ego. From the reference point of stillness, it was interesting to watch the ego playing out its fear.

Remember, the ego does not want to know it is powerless; therefore, it becomes defensive and resistant. Using affirmations, I began coaching my ego, giving it value as an important essential instrument through which the infinite "I" can experience this adventure.

I am telling you this story because there is an infinite and a finite part to every being. We can only experience oneness if our reference point of awareness is anchored in the infinite and not in the finite. If the ego or finite self feels that it has a purpose, that it is valued and safe, it stops resisting and becomes a transparency for Source. Hence, giving the ego value is an essential part of the game played within the collective. It took me a long time to coach my finite self to be an instrument for present stillness (Source awareness).

The ego wants to be the hero in the dream. It deludes itself into believing it can manipulate the reality it perceives, but does not realize that it, like everything else, is a program, an illusion that does not have real power of its own. Nothing in the perceptual reality of the collective is real or has power except for the power and realness we assign to it as expressions of Source. Anchoring our awareness in the present stillness of Source dissipates the grip of the ego's scream for attention. Present stillness allows us to see the world the way it is, as a reflection of the wholeness of being.

I have had an experience of oneness. It changed my life, but I have not been able to recapture it. Is there a reason for this?

Experiencing oneness is different for everyone. Some have less resistance than others. It all depends on our attachments, identifications, and associations with the images and forms of the material reality that we perceive as our world. Some people have sudden awakenings and then fall deeper into the conditioning of their realities, because of the fear associated with dying daily to the present moment of "now." Just the idea of trying to achieve an awakening experience creates resistance that divides and separates us even more, because in that moment, we are fully occupied with thinking and doing instead of *being*.

Awakening to Source awareness happens when we are ready for it. If we try to induce an experience of wholeness or oneness through hallucinogenic drugs, it could result in emotional, mental, or addictive imbalances. This is because we cannot experience oneness or wholeness if we do not realize that it is who we are. Trying to get there or attain it, or merge, align, or become one with it, means that it is separate from us and that we think we have to "do" or "think" something to achieve what we want.

There cannot be oneness and something else. There is only oneness. We cannot achieve it. It is already present in the here and "now" as everything perceivable. To be present in this awareness, we have to die every moment from the perception that we are the images and forms experienced through our minds' filters. Our insecure egos play the game of survival, holding us firmly in the illusion of separation, opposition, and resistance.

As we begin to wake up in this dream-adventure, we become aware of the interconnectedness of everything. A subtle trap that most of us fall into is trying to intellectualize oneness instead of experiencing it. Remember, we are not one of the many who makes up oneness. We *are* oneness, infinite consciousness—just expressed as an individual being experiencing a unique perspective of the collective mind. The ego cannot comprehend oneness because it sees its world as being separate from itself. Therefore, it only experiences division and separation. Only in present stillness, devoid of the activities of the mind, can we experience the nondual oneness of Source, the infinite *I*.

Life, Death, and Reincarnation

The soul is a powerful individualization of Source. It is a gathering point for consciousness that allows an entire universe of biological systems to evolve and develop within its field (aura), forming the corporeal vehicle. The organic material of the vehicle is made up of the elements within the collective mind (physical universe) in which the being evolves. Therefore, the vehicle has to be nourished and maintained by the organic materials of the life forms living within each specific collective.

Without the soul, the body cannot maintain itself or function as a sentient being. Every being has a specific window of time in which it exists in physical reality. The circumstances each individual exists in and the choices it makes influences its life-span.

When the soul detaches from the body because the vehicle is somehow damaged, diseased, or worn out, the corporeal mind unplugs from the collective in which it existed, leaving behind the vehicle (body) that then rapidly disintegrates. The once-focused substance of life, the soul, expands and returns to unfocused Source.

However, the memories of every individual being and every experience ever collected are stored and continue to exist within the collective mind. Imagine it like a massive, growing database. Certain people who have the right password can log in and access it. In other words, a person who is sensitive enough can focus and tune into a specific vibration of someone and is then able to review, for example, the highlights of an individual's life.

Just a reminder: everything exists within our individual consciousnesses. The physical universe, as we know it, is a living library of everything that has ever been. Through present stillness, we can access this library and explore anything we are interested in and focused on. However, we first have to attain its specific level of awareness before anything is revealed to us. Hence, great discoveries and clear insights happen in moments when we let go and allow present inner stillness to speak.

Source Cannot Die

Source cannot die; it only appears to change form through the filtered perceptions of the mind. In truth, no one dies. The substance of all life is infinite, omnipresent Source. No life disappears or goes somewhere. Only the physical forms and images within the collective dissolve, but the memories and impressions of every life continue to live within the collective mind multiverse.

The soul plugs into the collective mind to enable a physical experience to unfold. The collective mind exists within our consciousness, along with everything within our awareness, including every person we have ever known. Nothing exists or happens "out there" somewhere. Hence, just thinking of a person brings him or her into our present awareness.

In other words, if we recall a memory of a person, dead or alive, and experience that memory in the present moment, a contact is formed that connects us with our version and impression of him or her. It could even happen that we feel the person's presence if we sit long enough in present stillness. Remember, the person we are connecting with or recalling in our memory is the very same Source that we are. However, in our minds, we have fragmented Source and given it a form, image, and name, which we then identify as a specific person.

Just because the physical body is not present anymore does not mean the presence of the individual has disappeared. People continue to exist within our consciousness as memories of our complete or incomplete selves. They are all the same infinite essence that we are, except that they are not individual, focused points of Source anymore; they are unfocused Source, present in and as everything.

In our personal stories, every individual being within our awareness plays the role of a reflector onto which we project our own ideas and beliefs. Our memories of people are the stories we have attached to and believed in. If we have negative memories in which we resist and hate, or if we have unfinished relationships with anyone, we bond ourselves to that specific archetypal thought system within the collective.

This thought system holds us in a matching frequency where we keep meeting the same problems until we have transcended them. We only ever find ourselves reflected back to us through the people, places, and events within our specific collective. Remember, this is all happening within our individual consciousnesses. There is only Source expressing as every individual consciousness perceivable. Everything else is our stories.

When our present adventures are complete, we all return to the unfocused infinite Source, the substance of all life, light, and unconditional love. Our attachments to the forms, images, and ideas that we hold of people are what we mourn when they appear to leave the physical realm. While we are plugged into the collective mind reality, what we really see is just focused points of Source appearing in different suits. The suits may come, go, and leave us with memories, but Source does not change. Source is timeless, infinite, and omnipresent.

The Myth of Linear Reincarnation

When the body dies, the soul transforms from a focused point of consciousness back into unfocused, infinite consciousness. There appears to be a continuous contraction and expansion of Source. Each contraction into a focused point of awareness is a new awakening into a new life. Every expansion back into infinite consciousness is the end of an individual life adventure. This is all happening simultaneously in the present "now."

Remember, infinite consciousness only exists and expresses in the present moment. Our perception of time and space allows us to experience a linear perspective of reality within the collective mind program we are plugged into. Nevertheless, this all happens simultaneously in the present.

Source expresses simultaneously as every incarnated being. However, we are only consciously aware in one specific life at a time. There is no single continuity of an individual being reincarnating in a linear string of lives. This is a myth created by the ego's need for continuity.

Linear reincarnation is a mind-made idea, invented by the ego's need to survive within the collective mind. Only the ego perceives separation from everything else within its perception of time and space. Hence, out of the fear of death and the unknown, the ego creates a concept in which it has continuity, or maybe a new chance to make things right the "next" time. This is how and why the ego invented the ideas of heaven and reincarnation.

The soul is fully aware that it is a focused individualization of Source. It is also aware that, as Source, it appears as all existing souls simultaneously. The reason that we are only consciously aware and focused in one experience at a time is because it gives us the opportunity to explore the collective mind reality and all the adventures the different realms have to offer.

Some people cling to the idea of reincarnation because they hope the next life will be better than the one they are presently living. Many spend time regressing to "past lives" in the hope they might discover who they used to be. There are books, lectures, and workshops for seekers who are interested in these subjects. However, this brings nothing but an attachment to beliefs that distract us from the present "now."

In this present moment, we exist as all beings in all perceptions of time and space simultaneously. If we try to find out who we are in a parallel life, we only ever tune into the frequency we resonate at in this present moment from this particular point of awareness. We only ever find the awareness of ourselves staring back at us.

If we really want to know who we are in parallel lives, then all we have to do is to look at the people around us. Even if we shift our awareness to another frequency, we once again find that changed frequency of ourselves reflecting back to us.

How can I know this is all true?

Practice *being* present in stillness, and you will find all the proof and answers you are looking for.

Can one specific soul be split? Can one soul appear as separate people in different times (or simultaneously, as a group of beings)?

Yes, it can. Remember, time and space is a concept that only happens within the collective mind reality. Therefore, one specific soul could be focused and active in many different periods simultaneously, or in one specific period as a group of beings. Whatever the situation, these beings always feel connected with one another. This is often confused with linear reincarnation.

All of time and space happens in the present "now." Every soul can appear as one individual being or as many different life forms simultaneously. All beings are equally the same Source, each experiencing a unique, individual perspective of the whole.

Every individual life experience adds to the collective mind multiverse and is valuable—no more and no less than any other life. The essence of every life is you, not your ego's self (the material "me") but your infinite self —Source. There is no one single past lifetime, because everything is happening "now." We are all of these lives, whether we perceive them as in the past, present, or future through the collective mind experience.

The way we consciously choose to interpret the collective reality is how it appears to us. Death, disease, and suffering are all part of the perceptual reality within the collective mind story. It is all part of the adventure and the game called life.

When my wife suddenly died, my world fell apart. I miss her terribly. Where is she now?

She is with you and present within your consciousness every time you think of her. As infinite consciousness, she is present as all the colors of the sunset and the fragrant smell of a blossoming rose. She is the smile on all people's faces as they realize how wonderful they are. Even more, she is the unconditional love that allows life to continue as an adventure to remember. No one leaves or goes away. As memories, people stay with us, and as Source, they express as our world and us.

Spiritual Awakening

A spiritual awakening is a very different experience from an intellectual awakening. Through an intellectual awakening, we experience clarity and a deeper insight into something we've been focusing on. It is when a person who has been focusing on something specific has a revelation. Nevertheless, our reference point of awareness remains anchored in the ego.

In a spiritual awakening, we experience a paradigm shift that flips our perspective to a completely different reference point of awareness. This experience exposes us to a perspective of reality that does not always correspond to what we are used to or to what we know. As humans, we learn through repetitive behavior. This conditioning anchors our reference point of awareness in a specific way of thinking, doing, believing, and behaving. So, when our reference point of awareness shifts to the unknown, life could become weird or wonderful, depending on how we interpret or deal with the shift.

There are different ways in which a spiritual awakening can happen. For many it is a gradual experience, but if it happens suddenly, it can sometimes be difficult or problematic to deal with. If a person is not ready for the shift, the experience could result in confusion, insanity, loss, or possible suicidal tendencies, especially if he or she does not have loving support.

A spiritual awakening is a game changer in which the ego experiences the loss of its identity or the conscious transformation from dictator to instrument. This is usually a gradual process and takes time and commitment to integrate. However, it is possible that an awakening could happen unexpectedly or after a traumatic experience, an illness, or surrender to the constant stress and resistance within the collective survival game.

If we are ready for a paradigm shift awakening, the transformation of how we accept and allow change is smooth. For example, if we are already aware that we are the stillness behind our thoughts and mind activities, then awakening results in greater insight and experience. Some beings experience awakenings or paradigm shifts in stages. Shifting our reference point of awareness is not traumatic or confusing when we move through the change gradually.

It takes discipline and focus to shift from the ego's fragmented awareness of just thinking and doing to the stillness of *being* present as Source awareness. When thinking and doing happens through *being*, harmonious experiences unfold effortlessly.

Awakening requires a certain level of intelligence and an expanded perspective of awareness. It is also essential that the feeling faculties are intact. If we are desensitized, then it does not matter how intelligent we are; we will never awaken within the collective. Our feeling faculties are essential to the awakening process. All spiritual awakenings, regardless of how they happen, are experiences that result in clarity, expanded awareness, and a deeper insight of the wholeness of being and the interconnectedness of life. The key to awakening is to develop our awareness on all levels: spiritually, intellectually, and emotionally.

Love

Two important characteristics make up every human being. These are the *human animal* and the *consciously aware human*.

The human animal functions purely from the reference point of the physical body. It only experiences a fragmented world in which it needs to survive, defend itself, distribute its genes, and serve its own interests. All human beings begin their life cycles as human animals. As they evolve to greater levels of awareness and realize that everything in creation is interconnected and exists within their individual consciousnesses, they awaken as consciously aware humans.

The human animal can achieve a high level of intelligence, but it remains a self-serving animal until it has evolved beyond fragmented perceptual awareness. The human animal only understands conditional love and may love someone passionately one day but turn against that person the next day if his or her needs are not fulfilled.

Conscious humans experiences oneness because they are aware that the world as they see and experience it exists within their individual consciousnesses. Human animals who have evolved to the awareness of conscious human beings never participate in war or the malicious destruction of other humans. Conscious humans feel unconditional love because they have the awareness, experience, and understanding that all of life is interconnected. They know that every being within their awareness is a reflection of their complete or incomplete selves.

This makes the subject of love fascinating because unconditional love is the glue that holds everything together, whereas conditional love is a temporary, self-fulfilling and self-serving experience based on attachments, needs, desires, and survival.

With conditional love, when a person's needs have changed, shifted, or not been fulfilled as expected, love disappears or can flip over and become anger, rage, revenge, or abuse. However, both qualities of conditional and unconditional love exist within every human. Our level of awareness within the collective mind program determines whether we evolve from a human animal into a conscious human being.

At present, a large portion of the world's population is sitting on the border between both, fluctuating from one side to the other. The programming and conditioning within the game of the collective makes the transition difficult. However, surrendering to present stillness allows us to embrace unconditional love effortlessly.

Conditional Love

Most humans can only identify with the ego's experience of conditional love. The proof is all around us. If we have lived a so-called "normal" life, we have probably experienced this type of ego love many times over. The moment a situation in a relationship arises that we don't like, want, need, or agree with, our love dies and we move on to the next person who makes us feel warm and fuzzy.

Once again, this kind of love only lasts if our personal needs or desires are satisfied or fulfilled. If the situation changes again or we grow apart from partners because we develop different opinions and ideas about life without being able to find a compromise or balance, then the cycle continues. We only ever find our complete or incomplete selves reflected to us through the people we attract into our lives. The big question is, what do we learn from them? If we cannot recognize the wholeness and completeness within ourselves, then we cannot recognize it in someone else and expect them to fulfill the wholeness of our desire.

Conditional love is a wonderful example of how volatile life and relationships can be. How we shift and change as we search for fulfillment and completion is an essential experience that helps us to evolve. If we had been born into this world already fulfilled as conscious human beings, we would not need contrasting experiences or the adventure of an evolving life. Because we begin our physical adventure as human animals, we need the stimulation of constant change and contrasting challenges. Varied relationships and the experience of conditional love offers us many opportunities to grow and evolve.

Unconditional Love

Unconditional love is love without conditions, judgments, or attachment. At this level of awareness, there is no division, separation, or fragmentation. Hence, there are no demands, behaviors, ideas, or beliefs to follow. Unconditional love is the interconnectedness of all life; it unifies and is the glue that holds everything together.

Wholeness can only recognize wholeness. If we have our reference point of awareness anchored in unconditional love and the present stillness of infinite consciousness, everything we see and experience through the body's eyes will reflect the wholeness of being, the mirror of completeness.

Source expresses itself as the three qualities that allow all of creation to appear. These qualities are life, light, and unconditional love. Life appears through the mind as light. This living light becomes the images and forms of all creation. The abundance, prosperity, and wealth of life is Source expressed as unconditional love. Without the filters of the conditioned mind, we are aware of the interconnectedness of all life. Hence, we experience the wholeness of being and unconditional love.

> *I love my daughter unconditionally, but I do not like her husband and I cannot stand his family. Am I missing the true meaning of unconditional love?*

You have used the term "unconditional love" in the context of a focused relationship with someone. You love your daughter and are focused and attached to her, but not the others. This is conditional love.

The true meaning of unconditional love has often been misunderstood or confused with conditional love. We cannot have unconditional love for one being and not another. This in itself is an act of dividing and separating. Where there is division and separation on any level of awareness, there cannot be the completeness and unification of unconditional love.

How do unconditional love and stillness meditation fit together?

Combining the practice of unconditional love with inner stillness meditation is a powerful way to heal our lives on all levels. Practicing unconditional love starts with allowing, accepting, recognizing, and acknowledging the people and the world around us without any conditions. This is a form of giving. The love we project out into our world always flows back to us as abundance, prosperity, and health. Combining this with daily inner stillness meditation opens the heart center, which reveals the interconnectedness of all life and the harmony of the wholeness of being.

PART III

Living in the Dream Story

Filling the Emptiness

The corporeal mind's awareness is fragmented. Hence, it always feels like something is missing. We often relate to this as a feeling of emptiness that we constantly try to fill with achievements, rewards, material gain, drugs, various addictions, and belief systems. From the perspective of the ego, fulfillment is only ever experienced as a fleeting glimpse of wholeness. After the high, a low follows, and the search continues.

We spend much of our time searching for the magic recipes that will give us everlasting fulfillment. We search everywhere except within ourselves, within the present stillness of our inner being. Until we awaken from our egos' falsely perceived powers and its fragmented perspective of the world, we never fully realize that fulfillment and all the great treasures we could ever imagine already exist within us.

In the process of trying to fill our emptiness with the things of the world, we begin to worship the things of the mind. However, the mind can only conceptualize and create objects, images, and forms; it cannot give them life. Source is the substance of life. If we are disconnected from Source, we become empty and lost in the illusions of our mind-made stories.

Within a story, we only ever find more stories to identify with and attach to, but none of them will fill the empty space left by an unfulfilled life. Lasting fulfillment cannot be found in the story or through the things and activities of the material world. Fulfillment is a perpetual state of oneness and the awareness of the wholeness and completeness of being.

Do you think that if all the money in the world was shared, we would all feel more fulfilled?

The great wealth of a king or the poverty of a monk has never solved the search for fulfillment. Nothing in the mind-made reality of the material realm can be completely fulfilling. Fulfillment (or even happiness) cannot be bought with all the riches of the material world. Neither can starving, denying, or detaching from material objects result in everlasting joy or fill the emptiness. Fulfillment is a state of *being* that is experienced as completeness and the feeling of wholeness. This cannot be found in the temporary material illusions that make up the collective mind reality.

If this is true, and if it is as simple as you say it is, why are so many people lost, confused, and still searching for fulfillment?

The corporeal mind does not like stillness because it is terrified that it will lose itself. The only place we ever get lost or confused is in the perceptual world of the mind. The reason that people are still searching is that they believe the secret is "out there" somewhere in a concept, belief, or system. For most people, it is scary to search within and be present in stillness. However, here they will find all the answers and the fulfillment they are seeking.

Remember, present stillness does not mean you have to live your life in a quiet room. People confuse inner stillness with silence. You can have all the silence you want, but that does not mean you have inner stillness. Inner stillness is beyond the noise and activities of the mind and even the silence of a quiet environment or monastery. You cannot find it in a place, space, or idea, because it is not a concept. It is the true nature and center of every being. Everyone has the exact same inner stillness. There is not a different stillness center for each individual. There is only stillness present at the center of everyone.

Recognizing Ourselves in Everything

The physical life experience consists of many intertwining stories. Each one of us plays an important role by adding the experiences of our own stories to the greater collective. The compilation of all these stories shifts and expands the collective mind, thus allowing human consciousness to evolve to new and different levels of awareness. The catch is that the collective mind reality (physical universe) happens within our consciousness, not outside of us.

As Source—infinite consciousness, we are the stillness and awareness of everything. This is our true nature of being. The collective mind is Source in motion expressing as the light that forms and appears as all the universes, worlds, dimensions, and the programs within them.

For our infinite consciousness to experience a unique individual perspective of the collective mind, an individual, focused point of consciousness (the soul) is required. Everything exists and happens within our consciousness, including every person, concept, or thought. However, our corporeal minds can only grasp what appears through their conditioned filters. Hence, they only see and experience a fragmented world.

We unfold to our greatest unlimited potential when we realize that we are all interconnected. In other words, we are *one* with all that is. This is not a sudden revelation that happens by chance. It takes time for us to integrate and experience this way of thinking, feeling, and *being*.

However, it is essential to combine stillness meditation with the daily practice of feeling and recognizing ourselves in everything and everyone—every life form, object, or idea within our awareness. It is like the process of gathering more of ourselves. If we practice this with focus, intent, and unconditional love, it begins to heal the distorted filters of our mind. With dedication and practice, we become aware and begin to see the interconnectedness of the wholeness of being.

Just a warning and a reminder: an expanded awareness does not make everything we perceive nice and pretty. Once we begin to see the essence of every being, we become aware of their egos' stories and the games they play. Being awake is not walking around with a permanent smile on our faces and being nice to everyone, or letting abusive people walk all over us. Being awake within the dream means that we see the bigger picture and understand the game called life.

The ego's agenda is not always pretty, and sometimes we have to deal with other people's egos on the ego level. The difference is that we know their egos and projected images are not who they really are. We are aware that every person, regardless of agenda, comes into our lives as a reflector, messenger and teacher, but most of all, we have the awareness that behind their physical masks we are all the same infinite essence.

I still find myself judging and condemning different types of people who do not fit my definition of goodness. This makes me feel terrible. What can I do to shift this negativity?

Change how you associate with these people and look beyond the images and forms. You are still judging through the ego's conditioned perspectives and experiences. Remember that is just your version of the story. Acknowledge the essence of the being, not the ego and its mask.

We have to realize that what we focus on, accept, recognize, and acknowledge is how our experience in this life-adventure unfolds. If we focus on the thoughts and beliefs that limit, separate, or divide us, then we remain unconscious and unaware of the interconnectedness of life. In this state of limited awareness, we experience suffering and all that accompanies it.

When we shift our attention and focus to recognizing and acknowledging everything and everyone as being the one and same Source that we are, the interconnectedness and wholeness of being is revealed.

To function on this level of awareness, we first have to recognize that we are Source. Only then can we recognize and acknowledge it in every other person.

Living Consciously

We only awaken when we understand that everything we have and experience in this life flows through us, from us, and out into our world as the wholeness of being. This is living consciously. How we perceive and interpret our world is reflected back to us through the situations we find ourselves in and the people we attract.

Suffering is the epitome of believing that love, abundance, prosperity, and well-being come to us. This is the illusion of separation perceived through the filters of the fragmented mind. Nothing in life comes "to" us. Everything exists within our consciousness, so what we project out as our world flows "through" us. Therefore, how we interpret the collective mind we are plugged into determines how it flows through our consciousness and appears as our external reality.

If we focus on suffering, we become trapped in the darkness of a fragmented mind. Through practicing unconditional love and opening the heart center, we live consciously. This allows Source—infinite consciousness, to flow though us as the wholeness of being.

While we are focused and present within the corporeal vehicle, we have the opportunity to experience a great adventure within the illusionary realities of the collective mind-multiverse. The more aware we are that Source is our true nature of being, the more conscious we become of the game called life. In this way, we live consciously, and every experience of our journey becomes a joyous expression of gratitude. We are awake when we are aware that what we give to our world is what we give to ourselves.

To recognize and acknowledge the life and light of another being is to recognize the infinite self. This is living consciously. There is only Source—infinite consciousness. Everything else is our stories.

Live Your Passion

Until we awaken within the collective mind and realize it is all a dream, we will only ever experience glimpses of wholeness. If we have not yet allowed ourselves to be present in stillness long enough, the closest we get to experiencing completeness is when we live our passion.

To live our passion, we have to find the activities and work we love that fill us with joy and the feeling of completeness. Any form of doing and thinking expressed with passion allows us to experience a state of *being*. This state of completeness opens up the channels of joy that lead to fulfillment. This is living our passion.

If we have not yet found our passion, it might be that we are still stuck in the conditioning of the ego's separate self and its beliefs about survival. Those who have found and are living their passion always find themselves in the right place at the right time, where opportunities are abundant. If we are living our passion, the stream of life always takes us where we need to be. In this state of awareness, whatever we focus on unfolds in our reality, effortlessly.

> *I love my job, but the competition I am up*
> *against gives me second thoughts. What can I*
> *do?*

You might like what you are doing, but you have not found your passion yet. Remember, there is never competition if you are truly living your passion. There is only Source expressing a unique you.

Every being is different. The moment you think about competition, you have separated yourself and become a surviving particle within the masses with nothing unique to reflect and project out into your world. Live your passion through your heart center. *Be* present and centered in it when you express and do the things you love, and the right people will find you.

When we do what we love doing, the rest of the world that loves what it's doing finds us.

Everything Flows through Us

Remember, the collective mind is a vibrational reality that operates like a giant, interactive reflector, reflecting back to us what we are tuned into and what we project. Therefore, we can only ever find ourselves, just as we only ever give to ourselves. Nothing comes to us; everything flows through and then back to us through the same vibrational energy we projected.

If we believe we should suffer or that others are responsible for our pain and problems, then this is what we project out into the collective. In return, we get more of the same vibration reflected back to us through the people, places, and events within our awareness. If we believe that life is full of wonderful, helpful people who are there to help us on our adventure journey, so it will be.

When we do what we love doing, because we are focused and passionate, we enter a nonresistant state of being. This allows us to be in harmony with our world, which in turn opens up opportunities that reflect back to us through the collective as abundance, prosperity, wealth, and joy.

Unlocking Our Creative Reservoirs

As we awaken to realize that we are the stillness behind our thoughts, ideas, and beliefs, we begin to experience the interconnectedness of life. This unfolds for us a more fulfilling, peaceful, and loving existence. Present inner stillness is the key that unlocks the creative reservoirs of infinite consciousness.

If we are unaware of the incorporeal self, we can still tap into our inner stillness through focus, concentration, and living our passion. The act of thinking and doing through present *being* is a form of meditation in itself. In these moments of uninterrupted focus, when all random mind activities and distractions disappear, we open up to the stillness within. This stillness at the center of our passion, focus, and concentrated awareness is the center through which great knowledge, music, art, inventions, and creative ideas flow.

Concentration and focus become the avenue through which great artists, composers, scientists, inventors, and writers tap into the creative reservoirs of infinite consciousness. Their passion and intent allows infinite consciousness to flow through them as an expression of wholeness.

Many people have a natural or trained ability to focus and concentrate on one stream of thought while remaining undistracted by other mind activities. This is a skill that everyone is capable of learning, and it is one of the keys for developing heightened levels of awareness and increasing intelligence. However, not all great scientists or geniuses have an awareness or cognitive comprehension of the incorporeal self.

The reason for this is that their interest, intention, and focus are concentrated on the formation and workings of the external material reality. There are people who are not completely anchored in the material world; they have the awareness, faculties, and abilities to understand and comprehend the unseen or incorporeal worlds. Some people have a blend of both levels of awareness and can understand both corporeal and incorporeal realities with ease. These people are essential to the progress and change of the evolving consciousness within the collective mind.

Where Is My Joy?

The true experience of joy cannot be found somewhere "out there." It is right here, now, present within the heart of each one of us. Joy cannot be found in a person, place, or situation. Joy is Source expressing as unconditional love, flowing through us as the wholeness of being. In the moment when we experience real joy, our heart center opens, and we connect with all of life expressed.

Living in joy allows us to receive more love, success, prosperity, and wealth and to maintain a greater sense of well-being and physical health. Joy is fulfillment experienced. The reason it is so fleeting for most of us is that we have attached to and associated joy with an idea or belief. In other words, we have associated the true experience with an effect of something that might never happen. "I will be joyfully happy when..." This idea removes us from the present "now" where joy is actually experienced.

Joy is wholeness experienced and cannot be "found,"

because it comes from within. Joy is Source expressed as unconditional love, appearing as the abundance, prosperity, wealth, and harmony and the interconnectedness of all life. This is how the real experience of joy appears through the conscious mind of every person, anchored in the present stillness of Source awareness.

Finding Our Passion

Source has no purpose. Only the individual expression of Source, the soul, appears to have a purpose within the collective mind reality. This apparent purpose is to find fulfillment, to feel and experience the wholeness of being. However, finding our passion frees us from the constraints we experience within the collective mind. Living in our joy and passion allows our corporeal minds to be the instruments through which Source can express life, light, and love unconditionally.

Finding our passion is as simple as asking ourselves these five basic questions:

1. *What am I predominately focused on and thinking about when I feel happy, free, and at one with myself?*
2. *What do I love doing that brings me joy and*

allows me to feel happy?
3. *If I had a dream about what I would really like to do with my life, what would it be?*
4. *What job would make getting out of bed every morning an exciting adventure?*

What would I continue to do even if it meant giving up my free time?

Many of us find specific passions that we can focus on. However, many of us believe we cannot do what we love to do. Just this thought, and the idea of blaming our circumstances and limitations, separates us from our true nature of being. Source is no less in the poor than it is in the rich and prosperous. Buying in to the idea that we have limitations is recognizing and acknowledging to ourselves that life is a struggle. This way of thinking only creates more struggle, lack, and limitations.

Many of us forget that Source is present everywhere as every being in existence, as all the wealth and prosperity of the universe. Therefore, if we separate ourselves from Source, we separate ourselves from all the possibilities and probabilities available to us. If we go to Source or pray to it for help, healing, or money, then we reinforce the separation. Source does not fix or heal a problem for us. There cannot be Source and us, because Source is who we are. It is the true nature of our being.

We are infinite consciousness, expressing as all life.

Remember, finding our passion and anchoring ourselves in the joy of living through and from it is living in Source awareness. This changes thinking and doing to *being*. For example, brilliant singers or musicians allow their passion and love to flow through them. They are in a present state of *being* during performance. Mathematicians and scientists don't try to *think* an answer to a problem. They *become* solutions or answers as they flow through their consciousness within a moment of stillness and concentration. The artist or creative person is not trying to *think up* a design or an image. He or she *is* the design or the image as it appears on the canvas, paper, or computer screen. The same thing happens when we become consciously aware that we are infinite, omnipresent Source, expressing as the wholeness of being.

Forgiveness

The practice of forgiveness brings us into harmony with the complete self and returns us to wholeness. Forgiveness is an essential practice for all those who seek to heal their own suffering.

Everyone within our awareness is a reflection of our own complete or incomplete self. Remember, the collective mind happens within our consciousness. The situations we find ourselves in offer us the best ways to evolve and awaken within our perspective of the collective. In other words, they offer us challenges that help us to evolve on all levels of awareness so that we may remember that we are infinite consciousness.

Every experience is a piece of the puzzle. Our downfall happens when we attach to and identify ourselves by one piece of the puzzle without realizing it is just a small part of the bigger picture. This happens when we hold on to something from the past or point a finger and blame someone else for our misery instead of learning from it and understanding why it happened and why we drew it into our experience.

It is always easier to let go and forgive if we understand the agenda underlying the situation that haunts us. Carrying our misery with us is attaching and identifying ourselves with one piece of the puzzle. This is detrimental to our personal evolution. Hence, forgiveness becomes an essential and important part of assembling the bigger picture.

As I learned through my violent awakening experience, we only ever do everything to ourselves. The people we encounter along the way are messengers or teachers who reflect the vibrational frequencies we carry within us. Our programming and conditioning starts the ball rolling from an early age. Remember, the nature of our ego is dualistic. Hence, it is always comparing, judging, and analyzing what is good, bad, right, or wrong.

Forgiveness is part of the process of becoming consciously aware of the conflicting nature of the ego and the game within the collective mind reality. True forgiveness only happens when we are aware of the interconnectedness of all life. At this level of consciousness, we recognize that we do everything to ourselves.

In society, we often hear the words: "We should forgive but not forget." If we look around us, we see the evidence that forgiving but not forgetting has never helped to heal anyone. We should learn from our mistakes but not identify ourselves with them. Holding on to something from the past anchors us in a specific vibration. This prevents us from moving forward.

Forgiving is returning to wholeness. In wholeness,

there is nothing to remember or forget. Wholeness is always present and complete. The past does not exist, because there is only "now." Therefore, replaying and holding on to the memories of any event that happened in a specific period of our lives only reinforces fragmentation and separation.

If our perception of reality is anchored in victim consciousness, we identify ourselves with the suffering and trauma of our experiences. The problem with dwelling on our past issues is that it gives our egos a false sense of purpose in life. It shifts our focus and attention from taking responsibility for our present life and directs us to focus on pointing fingers and blaming someone else for our problems, issues, and shortcomings. For many victims, this becomes a full-time occupation.

Once we are stuck on this level of awareness, it is almost impossible to find inner stillness. It takes tremendous courage to surrender to the past and anchor ourselves in the present moment. To heal and pull ourselves out of this low-vibrating negativity, we have to recreate our associations with the person, place, or event. Part of recreating a new perspective is to learn and practice forgiveness and gratitude, because the two go together.

We cannot find fulfillment, completeness, or wholeness, while we resist, hate, judge, or condemn the fragmented and distorted projections we have attached to and identified with. We bond and attach ourselves to everything or everyone we judge or condemn.

The perceived problems and dislikes we cling to keep turning up in our lives in different forms. They appear as our obstacles, betrayers, enemies, or illnesses, but only until we realize that they are the outer expressions of our internal perceptions and resistances. Nothing really exists outside of us except for our programmed and conditioned perspectives on reality. Remember, the collective mind is a reflector, a giant, holographic mirror that can only reflect back what we project.

As aware human beings, we know that everything and everyone is interconnected. We are also aware that we cannot fix other people's problems, but we can forgive because we know how easy it is to be consumed by the ego's self-centered desires. No human is perfect. While we are conscious in a physical body, we are not only vulnerable to the natural laws and effects of the material universe but also easily influenced by controlling systems within the collective mind.

If another human is abusive or inflicts pain or suffering in any way, the important point to remember is not to make it ours; it is their pain that they are projecting on the people around them. Personalizing and owning this pain prevents us from developing our awareness beyond the ego's victim mindset.

Humans who have lost touch with their true nature of being often feel they can attain power through acts of abuse, inflicting pain, suffering, and other dehumanizing acts on others. In this state of unaware ignorance, the offenders eventually become the victims of their own perceived fragmented collective. The collective mind can only ever reflect back our own beliefs, hate, misery, and suffering. The abuse and suffering we inflict on people around us have boomerang-like effect and come back in unexpected moments or situations. We only ever do everything to ourselves, and what we do keeps us fragmented, separate, and divided from our true nature of being.

Projecting negative or hateful energy on a perceived enemy is like projecting it on ourselves. We are always our own enemy. There is no one out there except the projections of what we hold as truth within our consciousness. If we become a victim of someone's projected pain, it gives us the opportunity to awaken from the low-vibrating consciousness that we have been entertaining within our own mind. It is a wake-up call.

We always invite the incompleteness of ourselves to remind us where we are within the collective. It is easier to forgive if we have transcended the level of awareness we entertained when we believed we were victims. Forgiving ourselves for believing that someone else is responsible for our happiness or misery is an important stage of our personal transformation and frees us from suffering.

True forgiveness only happens when we have become aware of the interconnectedness of all life and when we have recognized the gift of the experience, regardless of how traumatic it was. Remember, the ego's personality is always going to behave and act out its conditioned beliefs, habits, fears, and anger as it tries to find fulfillment. If our conscious awareness of reality remains anchored in the ego, we will never realize that the true center of unconditional love and all the power in the universe is within us. Forgiveness dissolves resistance and allows us to find the stillness within our being. It is the first step toward healing the fragmented mind and returning to wholeness.

Gratitude

Gratitude is probably the single most powerful energy in this space-time reality, and it is the fastest and clearest path to being present in Source awareness. It is an act of giving, recognition, and acknowledgment. Just like forgiveness, gratitude reunites and returns us to wholeness.

Expressing gratitude toward another human by recognizing and acknowledging the wholeness of being within them is in itself a powerful way to heal not just ourselves, but also those whom we acknowledge.

Gratitude shifts how we use energy—from wanting and needing to giving. It is the recognition that life, light, and unconditional love flows from within us and through us as our external reality. Gratitude is an outpouring of creative energy. We experience it through the heart center, where all of life and the light and love we experience in the physical realm are connected. If we experience true gratitude daily, we continuously project positive and creative energy into our world and the collective mind reality we exist in.

Remember, in the bigger picture, we only ever do everything to ourselves. Genuine gratitude comes from the heart. We cannot fake it. If it is real, it returns as abundance, prosperity, well-being, joy, and love. This is the true essence of gratitude. It is like opening a path for our life force to flow through and then back to us. If we are truly grateful and express gratitude from our hearts' centers, the collective mind adventure unfolds as a harmonious experience.

> *I give a lot to friends, family, and strangers, but I sometimes feel that they are not grateful. This has become a concern for me. Is there anything you can suggest?*

If you are giving with the expectation to receive anything in exchange, whether it is recognition, reward, or acknowledgment, then you have missed the point of giving through gratitude. Giving with the agenda of getting something back is a typical attitude of the self-serving ego. We are all guilty of this, as it is part of our natural survival behavior. However, as we evolve in consciousness and experience the interconnectedness of all life, we are aware that what we give to our world is what we give to ourselves.

Life flows through us, then back to us. We experience gratitude because we receive love, abundance, wealth, health, and joy unconditionally. Gratitude is our way of recognizing and acknowledging the gifts, messengers, and love of our world. If we truly live in gratitude, then it is a natural reflex to give unconditionally.

If you are blessed within the game of life with abundance, wealth, and prosperity, then give those who are less fortunate the tools that will inspire and teach them to help themselves. Giving value to every being is the gift of healing our own lives. If you have very little material wealth, give by inspiring and uplifting people. Recognize and acknowledge the true power within them and show that they are valued and loved for who they are. Remember, we do everything to ourselves.

Accepting or Allowing

Acceptance is the first step toward transforming our perspectives and worldview. It is acknowledging that another perspective on reality exists apart from our own. We might not agree with it, but it is a step to opening up, growing, and expanding our awareness, which is all part of evolving to a higher level of consciousness.

The more we accept the differences in the ideas and beliefs of the people around us, the easier it is to connect, integrate, and become more aware of this wonderful life adventure we find ourselves in. Whatever we accept, recognize and acknowledge becomes part of our perceived reality, be it good, bad, or neutral. We are the directors of our adventures, and we decide and choose where to focus our energy. The consequences always present themselves along the way.

What we think and say we accept, acknowledge, and recognize does not always match how we really feel about something. Our preconditioned programming taints all of our judgments and influences how we perceive our reality. For example, a mother once told me that she could accept her child being gay, but deep down, she was still homophobic. This was because she was still harboring prejudices conditioned through her religious beliefs. Although she accepted her child, there were certain rules and boundaries attached to the acceptance. She just could not allow the flow of life to be the way it is. Her identification with and attachment to her beliefs created separation and division in her life instead of harmony and wholeness.

A couple of years later, this same woman told me how her life had changed when she finally realized that all beliefs are just programs we have accepted through the system we are trying to fit into. She now has a wonderful relationship with her son because she allows him to be the way he is without judgment.

All forms of prejudice and discrimination are an act of ignorance. Ignorance means that we lack awareness, knowledge, and information. It is all in the conditioning and programming we receive within the collective mind reality we identify with. As we awaken to realize there is only infinite Source expressing as all of life, we begin to realize that it is our own ignorance, lack of awareness, and our vulnerability to the collective mind's programming that make us believe we are separate from each other.

Accepting is recognizing, acknowledging, or tolerating another's perspective on reality, even if we do not agree or connect with it. When we say we accept something or someone, it does not mean that we have relinquished resisting it. The most harmonious and progressive choice is to allow everything to be as it is.

Allowing is removing judgments. It is seeing and experiencing the world through Source awareness. Allowing is to let everything be as it is, without the need or desire to change it.

Allowing is nonreactionary. It is recognizing and acknowledging the infinite in everything, allowing it to be what it is and knowing it is Source expressing as life. The ego might interpret it as good, bad, or neutral, but that is a personal perspective limited by conditioning.

By allowing, we do not acknowledge the ego's conditioned or programmed ideas and beliefs that it has attached to a person, place, or situation. Allowing shifts us beyond the ego's perspective of separation and returns us to wholeness and completeness, where everything is how it is. Judgment can only take place through the ego's perspective of a divided and fragmented world. Allowing reassembles our fragmented selves. It is the golden key to the interconnectedness of all life.

When and how do I find inner peace and present stillness in this conflicting world?

You will find inner peace and present stillness when you learn to love and allow those who do not love or accept you to be who they are without needing them to change. Every being within your awareness is in your consciousness. They are reflections of your complete or incomplete self. The incomplete aspect of you always hinges on how you interpret and judge the images and forms you perceive within your physical reality.

The completeness of you is always present as the wholeness of being. If you focus on recognizing and acknowledging the true essence of every being instead of focusing on the outer images and forms, you will begin to see and experience the wholeness in everyone. Remember, you only ever find the perception of yourself reflected back to you as your reality.

Visualization and Manifestation

I realized the power of visualization when I was in high school back in the 1970s, training for gymnastic competitions. Our coach had the radical theory that if we visualized our apparatus routines and felt the perfection of the movement, it would improve our performance. Naturally, our level of talent, focus, and commitment had a lot to do with the results of the different exercises. However, it made a huge impact on me, and I continued to use visualization and focus to manifest most of what I have achieved in sport and my professional career.

Visualization is the initial step of the creation process within the collective mind reality. In addition, our attitude, memories, and feelings play an important part in our daily manifestations. When we try to manifest something new and different, we are often disappointed when it does not happen on schedule. This strong emotional reaction of being disappointed turns out to be a barrier that prevents whatever we are trying to manifest from manifesting.

The idea that something did not happen sets up a memory of lack or the feeling of disappointment. From that moment on, whenever we attempt to manifest something, the memory of failure reminds us that it might not happen. If we try to manifest anything out of need or desperation, we always get more need and desperation. Remember, the collective mind reality is a mirror that only reflects what we believe about our world. Therefore, if we try to manifest out of lack and need, we receive more of the same. Incompletion can only recognize and attract incompletion. Wholeness can only recognize wholeness.

Life as we see and experience it within the collective mind, flows through us; it does not come to us. Nothing is "out there" somewhere. Everything happens within our consciousness. What we see, experience, and receive through the collective mind is the reflection of the complete or incomplete self. What we visualize and feel daily controls the steering wheel of our corporeal vehicles.

Visualization and feelings guide us through our life's adventures. If we run our vehicle on roads (memories) conditioned with lack, limitations, problems, and negativity, then life unfolds as a challenging, bumpy, and uncomfortable ride.

We can change the conditions of the road and the way we steer our vehicle by focusing on the wholeness and completeness of everything we imagine, think about, or visualize. This is an important part of awakening and expanding our awareness of the collective mind reality. Change, progress, and new experiences happen when we step out of our comfort zones and commit ourselves to new adventures. However, this will never happen if we have lazy and undisciplined minds.

The mind is the instrument for focusing, visualizing, and conceptualizing, but if we are not capable of using these abilities with intent, we are not able to manifest something deliberately. We may have fantastic imaginations, but without focus and intent, we cannot make anything happen.

Visualization and deliberate manifestation are essential parts of our existence as intelligent physical beings. However, it is important to remember that the mind is only an instrument and not the power behind the manifestation. The real power is our true nature of being, the substance of all life: Source, expressing and allowing what the mind visualizes to manifest.

When we realize that we are the stillness, the true power behind our thoughts, ideas, and beliefs, we become the creators of our own reality. Trying to manifest something is just a process of setting up an intention and focusing on its completion. Present stillness accelerates everything we set into motion through intent and focus. As we surrender to the present stillness of infinite consciousness, we realize there are no miracles, only deliberate manifestations.

How do I practice deliberate manifestation?

Practice your visualizations with intent, focus, and feeling. Remember, everything is complete, so in your visualization see and feel the reward, joy, and wholeness of the experience, and then be present and attentive in the emptiness of stillness. The longer you remain in this empty state without mind activities, the more effective your manifestations will be.

Remember, your world is within your consciousness. Being present and aware in stillness allows Source to express and configure the reality you visualize and focus on. However, your manifestations will always match the true core of your beliefs. If you have ridiculous or unrealistic goals and you do not actively participate in allowing them to manifest, then you will be disappointed. If you try to manifest out of need and desperation, your manifestations will match this belief of lack. You only ever get what you believe you are worth. Lack can only recognize lack.

The mind cannot create, because it is an instrument used to focus, visualize, conceptualize, and imagine, but it cannot give anything life that is not expressed through the essence of life itself—Source. If we hold the visualization with intense feelings of joy and accomplishment, it manifests as an expression of completion.

Healing

Everything is already present, whole, and complete. We are all the same infinite consciousness, present as the life, light, and unconditional love that expresses as the wholeness of being. As individual focused points of Source experiencing a physical reality through corporeal minds, we only perceive life through the filters of our egos' conditioned perspectives. These filtered perspectives delude us into believing that we lack completeness and wholeness in various departments of our lives.

Knowing that we are already whole and complete is the true art of healing. Wholeness is a state of awareness that has a healing impact on the corporeal vehicle. Remember, the corporeal vehicle exists in the perception of time and space and is affected and influenced by the collective mind. The physical reality is a temporary experience, not a permanent one. Disharmony and suffering only happens in the contrasting realities of the collective, where we attach to and identify with concepts and beliefs experienced through the corporeal vehicle.

In the realms of contrast, whatever we focus on becomes real to us. Hence, the collective mind reality consists of a multitude of beliefs and ideas, each offering a different perspective of reality and a unique adventure within the collective. However, the one thing that affects every incarnated being, regardless of scientific or religious belief, is the death of the corporeal vehicle. The body is always at risk, as it is a product of the environment, and it can quickly be affected or infected in many different ways. No one is exempt from physical death. Therefore, every life should be valued. Science, medicine, and various therapies can repair the body, but the true art of healing first happens in our consciousness.

So, if we are Source expressing as the wholeness of being, why do we get ill and diseased? Why do we age and die?

The answer is simple. Welcome to the collective mind reality, the realm of time and space, where physical life is a temporary experience. As corporeal beings, we are vulnerable to all the laws and rules within our universe. Life and death, health, disease, and aging are all part of the deal and the rules within the contrasting collective mind game.

If I awaken, do I still need to be concerned about my body?

Awakening and discovering that everything within the collective mind is a dream does not suddenly exclude us from needing tools—be they medicine, surgery, a prosthesis, or any help—to enhance our physical health or well-being. Whatever we do to live or feel better within our stories is to our advantage. Enjoy the adventure, because everything within the collective has a beginning and an end. Only Source—infinite, omnipresent consciousness—is always present and unchanged. Everything else is our stories.

Can a disease infect an enlightened person?

All beings within the collective mind reality are vulnerable to disease and death, no matter how evolved or enlightened they believe themselves to be. However, suffering and the trauma of disease are reduced when we are consciously aware that this life is a dream experienced within the collective mind reality. Suffering happens because we attach to and identify with our material stories.

The Importance of Feeling

We feel and experience the miracles and wonders of life through our sense faculties. Without them, physical life is an experience devoid of unconditional love, fulfillment, or real joy. Remember, feelings guide us and keep us present. While we are present and aware within physical bodies, our feelings inform us if we are in danger or in ecstasy.

If we are trapped in the programming of our intellects and shut off from our ability to feel the world around us, we are desensitized. In that state, we blur the line between intellectually understanding something and experiencing it.

For example, if we *think* we love someone, we are still speculating. The love has not yet transformed from an idea into an experience that we can feel. However, if we *feel* love for someone, we experience a deep and profound completeness and connection with the person. This experience affects our entire chemistry.

Another obvious example: we do not *think* we have an orgasm; we *feel* it, and we know without doubt when it happens. The point is, thinking about something is only speculating and is purely intellectual. However, feeling is a true experience that happens in the present moment.

Feeling happy is very different from thinking we are happy. The true feeling of happiness bubbles through us. Every cell in our bodies lights up as a healing and invigorating experience of wholeness. We cannot chase after happiness or try to find it, because happiness is the result of an experience that happens in the present moment. It is a state of awareness that opens us up to our true nature of being. People who genuinely experience the feeling of happiness radiate an attractive and positive energy.

Being present in Source awareness is not an intellectual experience, because we cannot be present in stillness by thinking about it. However, we can use the mind as an instrument to help, guide, and focus our attention on present stillness. Tuning the body-mind into *feeling through awareness* anchors us in the clarity of "now." This might take many years of practice and reconditioning our perspectives on reality, but the rewards and the newfound qualities we experience will be to our advantage.

Feeling through awareness or heightened sense awareness is commonly known as the intuitive sense faculty or "sixth sense." This faculty is the bridge between the incorporeal and the corporeal realms. If our natural awareness and feeling faculties (physical five senses) are desensitized through conditioning, specific belief systems, drugs, or medications, not only will we find it difficult to develop awareness through feelings, but it is also impossible to develop our intuitive sense faculties.

The Living Dead

Desensitization disconnects and separates us from Source and has therefore negative consequences within the collective mind reality. In this disconnected state of awareness, we become the prisoners of our conditioned beliefs, thoughts, and ideas. Without our intuitive feeling faculties, we never connect with the true center of inner being, which is present stillness. A desensitized person has no awareness of Source because he or she is consumed by mind activities and survival needs. Some even disconnect from their emotional bodies and become like the living dead. In this state of desensitized awareness, they function like human robots and vampires.

Human robots cannot feel empathy. They are conditioned to follow the programs designed by their keepers. With robots or cyborgs, everything is measured and analyzed as separate components of a materialistic reality. Life is not valued unless it is written in their programs. Everything is judged, rejected, or eliminated if it does not match the agenda or criteria of the system.

Human vampires live off the life force and energy of others because they are disconnected from their own. These humans are cut off from their emotions and have no empathy for other living beings. Their existence is superficial and self-serving and revolves around satisfying themselves at the cost of others.

If we are desensitized and unaware of who controls, conditions, and programs us within the collective, we become the robots and vampires of a nightmare dream world. Desensitized beings are servants to the players within the game of life. They never get to live and fulfill their own dreams.

Meditation

In Western societies, the practice of meditation is done in a variety of ways. These include breathing techniques, visualization, chanting mantras, and many forms of yoga or relaxation methods. Each method, technique, or approach has positive benefits if practiced with the right intent, focus, and discipline.

The goal is to be present, focused, and aware in stillness, free from the activities of the mind. Various techniques of meditation are beneficial for the practice of self-awareness and are effective in reducing stress. Being free of stress is important for health and well-being. Stress is the result of fear, and fear is the result of being under pressure or focusing on negative or distorted perceptions and perspectives that leave us with a sense of powerlessness.

Relaxation meditation and centering ourselves in the present "now" are an effective method for reducing stress. A relaxed and centered mind is more aware and alert. In this state, we are able to react and respond to situations without anger, agitation, or aggression. This helps us to deal with more of the stress and pressure of a domestic or working environment.

Meditation takes time, practice, and patience to master. It is the most effective and powerful self-awareness tool available to humans. Being present in the stillness of our true nature of being allows us to be whole again. With practice, it becomes more than just being still. It allows us to be the transparency through which infinite consciousness shines as the wholeness of being.

Returning to Wholeness

For the more advanced student, stillness meditation is a daily practice of being present in nonfocused Source awareness. The idea is to be a transparency for infinite consciousness. To *be* present in the state of nothingness means to be free of the ego's conditioned filters. This allows our true power to shine through.

In this state of being present, the mind becomes the instrument of awareness, free of the filters and the conditioned ideas of the collective. Here the mind is still and free of the judgments and the concepts of right, wrong, good, bad, or neutral. In present stillness, the mind allows clarity and completeness to present itself as the wholeness of being.

Meditation can help us to realize who and what we are. It can help us to tap into the unknown resources of the collective mind, or we can use it to rest in present stillness. However, until we have allowed our corporeal minds to be transparencies and instruments through which Source expresses as the completeness and wholeness of being, meditation on its own does not result in a life of fulfillment. To be truly present in stillness, we have to be free of resistance.

Harboring unresolved issues and problems sabotages many people from finding or unfolding to their inner present stillness. Using meditation to dissolve problems, diseases, financial, or relationship issues while still attached and identified with the conditioned filters of the mind does not work. We have to remember that the ego's fragmented perspective of the world holds the mind's conditioned filters in place. Unless we transcend these filters or shift how we interpret our world through them, nothing is going to change.

To transcend these filters, we have to realize that we are not the forms and images of the world but the stillness from which everything appears. Stillness is always present; it is what holds us together.

When we are not in meditation, it is our responsibility as sentient beings to recognize and acknowledge the wholeness in every life present within our awareness. This exercise in itself brings up many unresolved and hidden issues that we have to reevaluate and then reinterpret before we are able to heal our fragmented perceptions of the world. The mind resists change, so we have to prepare it to become an instrument through which we can experience completeness and wholeness.

Meditation is an essential tool for developing awareness and resting in the present stillness of infinite consciousness. However, we have to carry this inner stillness with us consciously and make it the center from where we see and experience our world.

Living through the Heart Center

The only way to break the cycle of suffering within the game is to awaken to Source. If we have questioned our thoughts and beliefs thoroughly, we will eventually realize that they are just stories we have attached to so that we can claim credibility or have something to identify with. We have to reach the awareness that we are the infinite stillness from which our thoughts and our world arise. At this level of awareness, we participate within the mortal games as conscious players. This frees us from the limitations and suffering that the corporeal mind experiences within the collective.

Living with our reference point of awareness anchored in present stillness (Source awareness) is being consciously aware that the collective mind exists within our consciousness, not outside of it. In other words, we are the awareness (Source) of the dreamer (soul) that is dreaming a dream (individual body-mind) within a dream (collective mind).

Source—infinite consciousness, is the stillness at the center of all that is. Present stillness is the key to experiencing the wholeness of being or heaven on earth.

Our inner stillness is the same center that is present as the center within every other being. *Being* present in our inner stillness unplugs us from the chaotic filters of the collective mind reality and opens the heart center. The effects we experience when living through the heart center are harmony, balance, prosperity, and well-being on all levels of awareness.

The heart center is the central point of our being where consciousness gathers and where Source focuses as an individual point of awareness. It is the center for our intuition and from where we experience unconditional love. From here, the physical life adventure begins with the first beat of the physical heart and ends with the last one.

It is through the heart center that we connect with all of life. The catch is, we cannot trick ourselves or pretend we are living through it when we are not. We cannot open the heart center or even begin to evolve to a higher level of awareness if we are functioning in a reality perceived through ideas that divide and separate.

A mind that induces or supports suppression, suffering, and war and destroys for self-gain, power, and glorification remains anchored in the limited awareness of the ego. As fragmented egos, we are not aware that what we do to others, we do to ourselves. The ego's awareness is limited to survival, reproduction, self-gain, and personal security. It cannot experience illumination or the wholeness of being because it has imprisoned itself by attaching to and identifying itself with the limitations of a perceived corporeal reality.

Opening and living from the heart center does not mean we have to try to use our minds to think better thoughts (although this is how we start the unfolding process). It also does not mean denying the body-mind world, changing our diets, or living in a cave. Opening the heart center is living in Source awareness. This is being present and aware within the infinite stillness of every life form.

From the place of stillness, we experience illumination and the completeness of all that is. In the past, only a few humans developed the discipline to do this. In the ancient world, these people became the masters and wise men who wrote and taught the timeless wisdom teachings that to this day are still relevant and necessary for the existence of harmonious human life.

At present, more humans are educated, awake, and aware and are able to focus with more intent. For this reason, greater levels of awareness will begin to unfold within the collective mind. Many of us who are only aware of the ego's materialistic reality need proof generated from a system of thinking that we rely on for our perceived purpose of existence.

The mind can only recognize itself. Source can only recognize itself. The mind and everything within it exists within Source. Therefore, we have to lift our level of awareness beyond the collective mind activities and anchor our awareness in present stillness—Source—before we are able to recognize and experience the incorporeal consciousness expressing as the wholeness of being.

We all have the innate ability to know everything we ever want to know. All knowledge, answers, and solutions are closer to us than we think. Everything is within our consciousness and can be accessed through present stillness, the core essence of our being. In this no-space, no-place, no-thing, we unplug from the collective mind reality and unfold to the presence that is present as all that is.

The Key

You are Source—infinite consciousness, expressing as an individual being. Within the perception of time and space, your unique experience gives you the chance to dream the best adventure you can. If you are not aware that you have this opportunity, the systems within the collective mind dream become your masters.

The key is to know that you and everyone within your awareness is incorporeal Source. You are one infinite consciousness, appearing as the billions of life forms you perceive through your individual corporeal mind. However, you can only be consciously aware in one experience at a time. Every being perceived within your awareness is a reflector of your wholeness or incompleteness, of your prosperity, love, and compassion or your hate, fear, prejudice, anger, greed, and poverty. Your enemies are always within your consciousness, never somewhere else. You cannot run away from yourself, because as infinite consciousness, you are present as everyone.

As individual focused points of Source, we are the central suns of our own universes, not as physical bodies, but as individual representations of Source. The body is merely the vehicle through which we experience the collective mind reality. We are Source, present as all the probabilities and possibilities conceivable. Therefore, as individual representations of Source, whatever we shine our light on lives in our awareness.

Source is the only power. For the mind to be an instrument and transparency through which Source can shine, we have to shift our reference point of awareness beyond the filters and activities of the corporeal mind to the present stillness of our inner being. This is the only way we can break the hypnotic trance of the systems and controls within the collective mind game.

Present stillness is the same zero point that exists as the center of every living being. In this stillness, there are no concepts of duality, limitation, need, disease, or conflict; there is only the completeness of the wholeness of being.

Be present and aware within the stillness of your inner being. You will find all the proof you need through your own experience. Remember, in essence, you are the ocean, not only the individual wave. We are not fragments or parts of Source; we *are* infinite Source, present here and now. Once we know we are Source—infinite consciousness—the game of life changes in our favor, and life unfolds as an endless adventure.

Conclusion

*What was the most difficult thing you have ever
had to learn?*

By far the greatest and most difficult challenge I've had
was to learn to allow and love unconditionally. I could
only begin to do this when I discovered that I am the
stillness out of which my thoughts, beliefs, and
perceptions of the world appear. It was in this moment
that I realized that we are Source—infinite
consciousness. Everything else is our stories.

NOTES

NOTES

NOTES

NOTES

www.ingramcontent.com/pod-product-compliance
Lightning Source LLC
Chambersburg PA
CBHW071754090426
42737CB00012B/1810